GW00402175

Microsoft

WINDOWS®
Survival guide

**Become a Windows expert
and get the very best
from your computer**

INCLUDES
Microsoft
Windows *Me*
Millennium
Edition

Paul Wardley

Prentice
Hall

An imprint of Pearson Education
London · New York · Toronto · Sydney · Tokyo · Singapore
Madrid · Mexico City · Munich · Paris

PEARSON EDUCATION LIMITED

Head Office
Edinburgh Gate
Harlow CM20 2JE
Tel: +44 (0)1279 623623
Fax: +44 (0)1279 431059

London Office:
128 Long Acre
London WC2E 9AN
Tel: +44 (0)20 7447 2000
Fax: +44 (0)20 7240 5771
Website: *www.informit.uk.com*

This edition published 2001
First published in Great Britain in 2000 by VNU Business Publications

© VNU Business Publications, 2001

ISBN 0-130-61231-6

The right of Paul Wardley to be identified as author of
this work has been asserted by him.

British Library Cataloguing-in-Publication Data
A catalogue record for this book is available from the British Library.

10 9 8 7 6 5 4 3 2 1

Edited by Mick Andon
Design by slowcat (info@slowcat.com)
Illustrations by Spike Gerrell
Typeset by Pantek Arts, Maidstone, Kent
Printed and bound by Rotolito Lombarda, Italy

The publishers' policy is to use paper manufactured from sustainable forests.

WINDOWS SURVIVAL GUIDE Contents

About the author

Paul Wardley, paul_wardley@hotmail.com, served his time as a programmer, college lecturer, computer systems administrator and technical editor of *What PC?* Having been released for good behaviour he now develops training resources, writes for several computer magazines, is a regular contributor to Computer*active* and works as a consultant specialising in training and education. It is his ambition to find time to build his own website.

Getting started

It's surprising how quickly you can learn to use a PC, even when you've never encountered anything like one before, but this is more a tribute to human adaptability than good design. Experts talk about how today's PCs and their operating systems are easy to use and intuitive, but try telling that to a person who has never used a mouse before and finds that when they try to click the left mouse button all their fingers twitch together. Ask someone who has never used a keyboard whether computers are easy to use. Is it 'intuitive' that two keys are needed to make a pound sign, that one type of slash should be called forward and the other backward, and that there's no division symbol on a keyboard despite the presence of several other keys with strange squiggles nobody ever uses?

Different ways of working

This book is for you if you've overcome such initial stumbling blocks and managed to turn your PC into a practical tool and a means of entertainment. Perhaps you use it write letters and reports, store pictures, produce home-

work projects, run clubs and businesses from home, play music, watch movies and send email, but despite these successes you have niggling doubts. You wonder whether you're doing something the way it ought to be done, and worry that you're not making the most of your expensive toy. When you've read this book you'll know that there's no such thing as the *right* way to use Windows.

For the price of an evening out you can buy a comprehensive multimedia encyclopaedia that would cost thousands of pounds in a print version. The massive potential market for Windows software leads to high-quality, low-cost software.

1

You probably know more than you think

One example of how Windows offers a choice of working techniques is that it's easy to think of four quick and easy ways of copying a file onto a floppy disk. Each is as good as the next and everybody can use the way they feel most comfortable with. If you know one way of doing it, you really don't need to know the others, but if you do you'll be able to choose a technique that fits in with whatever else you happen to be doing with Windows at the time.

We hope this book introduces you to some new techniques, and that you'll find them useful alongside the ones you already know. With luck you'll also become more aware of what's possible with Windows and what you can look forward to in the future. Just for the record, the four alternative ways of copying a file onto a floppy disk are:

● use **Copy** and **Paste** on the Edit menu of Windows Explorer
● use the shortcut copy and paste keys (**Control-C** and **Control-V**)
● drag the file onto the floppy disk icon displayed in My Computer
● right click with the mouse and select **Send To Floppy (A)**

How Windows began

The original Windows was not a great success and neither was its successor, which was called Windows 286, and was named after the 'power' processor of the day, Intel's 286. Windows 3.0 came out at just the right time in 1990 to capitalise on a new Intel processor, the 386. The introduction of the 486 and competition from rival chip maker AMD had led to drastic reductions in the price of PCs with 386 processors. They became affordable to ordinary home PCs and had the power to run Windows properly.

The big attraction of Windows was WYSIWYG – what you see is what you get. Until then the top-selling programs displayed typewriter-style text on a plain back-

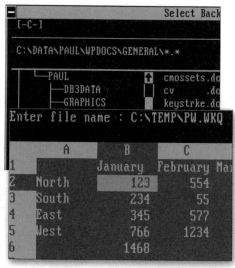

Not only did MS-DOS programs look boring, they were difficult to learn and you could only use one at a time!

Windows 3.1 had no Desktop so users tended to keep all their programs in Program Manager, which was controlled by menus. Because monitors had smaller screens than they do today it was common to run programs in full screen mode, switching between them only when absolutely necessary.

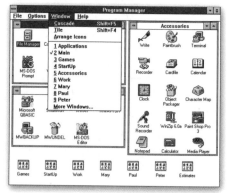

ground and users had no way of knowing what a finished document would look like until they printed it. Even desktop publishing was carried out by inserting formatting codes into text documents, so Windows was a revelation.

The benefits of a graphical user interface or GUI (say 'gooey') are the same now as they were then. As well as seeing exactly what your finished documents will look like when printed (or sent as an email or displayed on the web) you can work on them more effectively by using the mouse as pointer to click buttons and work controls, or as an on-screen hand to drag things into position.

Just as Microsoft was fortunate with the timing of Windows 3.0, the company again struck gold when the launch of a much-improved version 3.1 coincided with a fall in the price of 486 processors, and it was third time lucky when Windows 95 hit the streets just as the Pentium processor became cheap enough to use in home PCs. In retrospect it seems that half the country's computer users upgraded to Pentiums so they could run Windows 95, while the other half bought Windows 95 because they'd already bought a Pentium PC and wanted something to do with it. Either way it was good news for Microsoft and Intel.

Windows comes of age

Windows 95 was very different from Windows 3.1, having been designed for powerful PCs with good graphics, plenty of memory and big hard disks. Woe betide anybody who tried to run it on older machines designed for MS-DOS. Microsoft had by then stopped developing DOS, the product on which its initial success had been based, and the only people writing programs for it were software designers who found Windows 95 too slow for action games.

Windows 95 was good, but by no means perfect. Half-way through its life Microsoft introduced an upgrade incorporating many bug fixes and improvements. The upgrade was supplied only with new PCs and

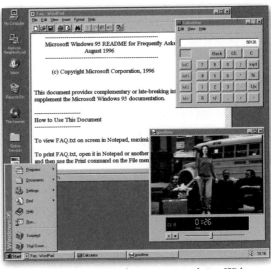

The Desktop in Windows 95 was a revelation. With not a menu in sight and programs filed away on the Start button (but always within easy reach) Windows at last had a work surface. The mouse became as important as the keyboard for manipulating objects on the screen.

couldn't be bought in the shops and was officially called Windows 95 OSR2 (OEM system release 2). If you bought a PC in 1997 or 1998 you might well still be using it. You can tell by right clicking My Computer and looking in the System Properties box. If it says Windows 95 4.00.950 then you've got the original version. If it says 4.00.950B you've got OSR2.

The B after the version number indicates OSR2, the mid-life revamp of Windows 95. Very late versions of Windows 95 had support for USB peripherals and were given a C suffix.

3

Windows becomes a family of products

Windows 95 OSR2 was strictly an interim measure until a new Windows was ready for release. When Windows 98 eventually arrived it was worth the wait. Many new features were added to the operating system, including USB support (see p91), better Plug and Play, slick multimedia and an internet browser built into the Desktop.

But after a year Windows 98 was itself in need of a mid-life kicker, which came in the form of Second Edition. This time Microsoft made the upgrade available to the general public but not many people bought it because all the bug fixes and enhancements it contained were already freely available on the Windows website. You can find out whether you've got Windows 98 Second Edition by looking at the System Properties box (see previous page) or by examining the opening screen of Windows Help. Easier still, look at the cover of the manual or the CD-ROM itself, both of which should be marked Second Edition.

New kids on the block

Released in September 2000, Windows Me (Millennium Edition) is the version people are wondering whether they should buy, which is why we've devoted a whole chapter to it, starting on page 80. There are other references to it throughout the book, especially where its features are significantly different from those in Windows 95, but it's essentially just a smartened up, streetwise Windows 98. Given the naming conventions of its predecessors you might be wondering

Windows Me (Millennium Edition) is slicker and easier to use than Windows 95 and Window 98, but the emphasis is on multimedia and innovation rather than data security.

why Windows Me isn't called Windows 2000, and the answer is that there's another Microsoft product with this name. Windows 2000 is the new designation for Windows NT, which is the corporate version of Windows designed for use on big networks. Windows 2000 is faster and more reliable than the home versions of Windows but less flexible. It doesn't do games, multimedia and entertainment very well and it's awkward to set up. The really big news is a completely new version of Windows, codenamed Whistler, that promises to combine the versatility and ease of use of Windows Me with the speed and reliability of Windows 2000.

Windows 2000, the corporate version of Windows, eschews change in favour of rock-solid reliability. The next version of Windows is said to combine the virtues of both systems in a common core.

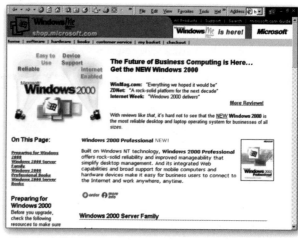

Whistler is promised for the end of 2001 which, given Microsoft's past performance in meeting product deadlines, might mean some time in 2002. For the foreseeable future you either stick with the Windows you've got or upgrade to Windows Me.

Getting the best from this book

If you decide to remain loyal to Windows 95 or Windows 98 this book can help. It tells you how to configure Windows for maximum performance, is full of tips on how to get more out of it and offers help in diagnosing and fixing common problems – just in case.

There are workshops at the end of each chapter, but we've followed a hands-on approach throughout so we advise you to read the book while sitting at your PC. Every technique we describe works with Windows 98, and nearly all of them with Windows 95. We point out where there's a difference.

You don't have to read the book from beginning to end, you can skip to the bits that sound most interesting, but note that in the earlier chapters we give you what are virtually click-by-click instructions for relatively simple tasks. Later, because we don't want to bore you with needless repetition, we make the assumption you can perform the same tasks with fewer instructions. Opening the Windows Control Panel is a good example. When it's properly introduced on page 7 we tell you where to find the Control Panel, what it does and how to use it. When we return to it later, as we do several times, we simply tell you to open the Control Panel.

A warning

Some of the techniques described in this book could cause Windows to stop working if you get them wrong. We haven't included anything beyond the capabilities of an inter-

PCs are as much about fun as they are about productivity, and with Windows it has never been easier to get so many different pieces of hardware and software working together. Nevertheless, as with any expensive system, it pays to learn how to take care of it.

ested and intelligent average user, and there's nothing that will damage the hardware in your PC or cause any permanent harm, but we don't want you to lose any important documents or have to spend hours reinstalling Windows.

Please follow our advice regarding precautionary measures, backups and copies when given. You can't rule out an unexpected power cut or a blown fuse which can confuse the best-laid plans.

CHAPTER 1

Preparing for action

When you buy a new PC it comes with Windows pre-installed on the hard disk, but computer vendors don't install every feature of Windows. They choose what they think people need. Their selection is based partly on the hardware they've built into the PC but mostly on what the experts at Microsoft have decreed is a typical installation. This includes everything you need to run programs and use the internet for web browsing and email, but it doesn't include many of the 'fun' features such as games, sound schemes and colourful Desktop themes.

Are you a typical user?

Surprisingly, a typical installation of Windows also leaves out useful tools such as Backup and Character Map. Backup does exactly what its name implies, and anybody who uses a PC for business and doesn't keep backup copies is asking for trouble. Character Map is a handy tool that everybody needs at some time or another to insert symbols or characters from foreign alphabets into letters and other documents – and these are just two of the many programs missing from a typical installation.

Whether you're working on a brand new PC or a machine that's so old you can't even remember what was on it when you bought

it, the first step in setting up a better Windows system is get rid of the bits you don't need and install the bits you do, which, along with setting up your hardware, is the theme of this chapter.

The Windows 98 Welcome screen pops up every time you switch on. When you've had enough you can banish it forever by clearing the tick in the bottom left-hand corner and then clicking the Close button.

What's on your PC?

To find out what is and isn't already installed on your PC you could browse through the programs on the Start Menu but it's easier to use the Add/Remove programs feature in Control Panel because you can also install programs from there.

Take Control

The Control Panel is the first point of access for many Windows features so it's worth remembering how to find it. Click the Start button and highlight the word Settings. This causes a menu to slide out, and on this you click Control Panel. Once the Control Panel is open you can start any of its features by double clicking a name or icon.

When you double click it causes the Add/Remove Programs properties box to appear. To view the optional Windows components click the Setup tab. If it takes a few seconds for Windows to work out what has and hasn't been installed; be patient. Eventually you'll be presented with a list, next to each entry of which is a tiny box. A tick in a white box means a component is fully installed, no tick means a component has not been installed, a tick in a grey box means there are several related components in this category and only some of them are currently installed. Double click any item (or use the Details button) to see what the hidden components are.

Choose your weapons

Tick any items you want to install and remove the tick from items you think you don't need. If you change your mind you can come back and make changes later. As you select the components to be installed, Windows tots up how much space they'll need and tells you how much is available on the hard disk. When you've made your choices click the OK button and have your Windows CD-ROM ready because you'll be asked to insert it.

Over the page is a table listing the optional components in Windows 95, 98 and Me. There's a brief description of each, but to find out more you can type the name of any feature into Windows Help.

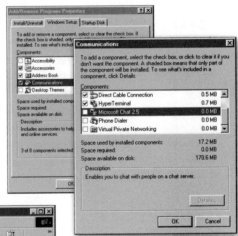

The grey-shaded tick box next to Communications shows that it contains several components but that not all of them have been installed. Double clicking Communications reveals the components available and those already in place.

Every computer's Control Panel is slightly different, being tailored to the hardware inside. This one, from a notebook PC, has Infrared and PC Card controls you don't need on a desktop PC.

7

Optional Windows components

Component	What it does	Installed? 95	98	Me
Accessibility Options	Keyboard, sound, display and mouse features for people with impairments	Y	Y	Y
Accessibility Tools	Magnifier and high visibility cursors	X	N	Y
Address Book	Contact management	Y	Y	Y
Audio Compression	Essential for recording and playing sounds	Y	Y	Y
Backup	Backs up hard disks or individual files	N	N	N
Briefcase	Makes it easier to synchronise files between a desktop and laptop PC	N	N	N
Calculator	Mathematical calculator	Y	Y	Y
CD Player	Plays audio CDs	Y	Y	X
Character Map	Inserts symbols and foreign characters into documents	N	N	N
Clipboard Viewer	Shows you the last item you have copied	N	M	N
Compressed Folders	Make and use Zip files in Windows Explorer	X	X	N
Desktop Management	Services for system administrators on networks	N	Y	X
Desktop Themes	Customised backgrounds, wallpaper, sound, icons and more	X	N	N
Desktop Wallpaper	Images and pictures for the Windows Desktop	N	N	N
Dial-Up Server	Connect directly to your PC via modem	X	N	Y
Dial-up Networking	Connect to the internet via your modem	N	Y	Y
Direct Cable Connection	Connect two computers using serial or parallel cables	N	N	N
Disk Compression	Adapts a hard disk to make it hold more data	X	N	N
Document Templates	Ready-made documents	Y	Y	Y
Drive Converter FAT32	Provides more usable space on large hard disks	X	Y	X
Games	Have fun – titles vary with each version	N	N	Y
Hyper Terminal	Connect to non-internet computers via your modem	Y	N	N
Imaging	Import, view and annotate pictures	Y	Y	Y
Internet Connection Sharing	Share one modem between multiple PCs (on a network)	X	N	Y

Key
Y = Installed
N = Not installed
X = Not available in this version of Windows

The components listed here are arranged in alphabetical order. In the Add/Remove Programs section of Control Panel they're presented in functional groups such as Communications, System Tools, Multimedia and so on. Over the years some of the components have switched allegiances so that, for example, Clipboard Viewer and Character Map have been promoted from being mere accessories to system tools, which is why we haven't attempted to group components in the table in any way.

Backup and WordPad are special cases. In Windows Me, Backup is no longer installed from the Control Panel. You install it instead directly from the Windows Me installation CD-ROM where it can be found in a folder called Add-ons\MSBackup. WordPad has been promoted in Windows Me from being an optional component to being an integral part of Windows, so you get it whether you want it or not.

Optional Windows components

Component	What it does	Installed? 95	98	Me
Media Player	Play audio and video clips	Y	X	Y
Microsoft Chat	Access to chat servers on the internet	X	N	X
Microsoft Fax	Send and receive faxes	N	X	X
Microsoft Network	Microsoft's own internet service	N	Y	Y
Mouse Pointers	More pointers for your mouse	N	N	Y
MS Wallet	Secure payments over the internet	X	N	X
MSN Messenger	Exchange live messages with your friends on the internet	X	X	Y
Multilanguage Support	Set up Windows for other (mainly European) languages	N	N	N
Multimedia Sound Schemes	Sounds you can attach to Windows actions and events	N	N	N
Net Meeting	Work simultaneously with others via internet or local network	Y	Y	Y
Net Watcher	Monitors network connections	N	N	N
Online services	Selected online service providers	X	Y	Y
Online User's Guide	CD- or disk-based user guide	N	X	X
Outlook Express	Email and news program	X	Y	Y
Paint	Create and edit bitmap images	Y	Y	Y
Personal Web Server	Use your PC as an internet server	X	Y	X
Phone Dialer	Dial phone numbers using your modem	Y	Y	Y
Quick View	View files without opening them	N	N	X
Sample sounds	Sounds to attach to Windows actions and events	N	N	N
Screen Savers	Pictures to amuse onlookers when your computer is unattended	Y	N	Y
Shockwave	Plays Macromedia Director files	X	Y	Y
Shockwave Flash	Plays Macromedia Flash files	X	Y	Y
Sound Recorder	Record voice and other audio files	Y	Y	Y
System Monitor	Monitors system performance	N	N	N
System Resource Meter	Displays memory resources used by Windows	N	N	N
Universal Plug & Play	Lets PCs share Plug and Play hardware over a network	X	X	N
Video Compression	Essential for recording or playing video files	Y	Y	Y
Virtual Private Networking	Secure private chats over the internet	X	N	N
Volume Control	Adjusts sound output	Y	Y	Y
Web Enterprise Management	Remote tools for use by system administrators	X	N	X
Web Publishing Wizard	Publish your own home pages to the web	X	N	Y
Web TV	View selected Internet pages using only a TV tuner	X	N	Y
Win Popup	Send pop-up messages on a network	Y	Y	Y
Windows 95 Tour	Overview of Windows 95	N	X	X
Windows Messaging	Email and faxing for Windows 95	N	X	X
WordPad	Simple word processor	Y	Y	Y

Adjusting keyboard and mouse responses

Now that you know where the Control Panel is (see page 7) you can use it to customise the way your mouse and keyboard work. Many people feel that when a key is held down it should repeat faster than it does as standard, and nearly everybody has problems getting Windows to recognise whether a mouse has been single clicked or double clicked. Fortunately, you can teach Windows your typing and clicking styles.

Keyboard capers

Double clicking the Keyboard icon in Control Panel brings up Keyboard Properties. The important tab is labelled Speed. On it are two slider controls. The

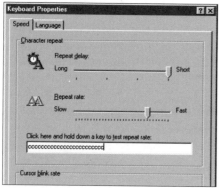

Adjusting the keyboard repeat rate has a knock-on effect on the speed at which the cursor keys operate, so choosing the right repeat rate can make it easier to scroll through spreadsheets, web pages and long word processed documents.

top one determines the delay before a key starts repeating, and the one below it the speed of the repeat. Try minimising the repeat delay by moving the top slider all the way to the right.

By default the bottom slider control is centred, which produces a rather sedate repeat rate, but most users prefer the slider to be positioned somewhere to the right of centre. There's a box in which you can sample different repeat rates but you'll get a better

The Windows Me Mouse Properties box contains a control called ClickLock, which offers an easier way of dragging an object and selecting text for those who find it hard to hold down a mouse button and move the mouse at the same time.

idea if you try navigating around a long document in WordPad or any word processor.

Mouse traps

Windows 95 won't recognise a mouse with a central scroll wheel unless you install special drivers supplied with the mouse. Windows 98 and Windows Me can automatically sense and respond to a wheel rodent.

Fortunately, the mouse setting that's most important if you are to use your computer smoothly and fluently – its double-click speed – can be adjusted in every version of Windows. To set the double-click speed highlight the mouse icon in Control Panel and choose Open from the File menu. In the test area is a child's toy. Adjust the double-click slider (by moving it towards the slow setting on the left) until Jack jumps out of the box even when you double click at what you regard as your slowest speed. In this way your clicks will be recognised even when you're tired or under the weather. While you've got Mouse Properties on the screen, why not take a look at the other options it contains?

File names

Everything on the hard disk of a PC is saved as a file, whether it's a program, a document you've created yourself, a picture downloaded from a digital camera or the high scores of a game. When you create your own files you give them names like 'Letter to Ann' and 'My CD collection' to make them easily identifiable, but behind the scenes there's a lot more going on.

Every file name has two parts: the one you give it and a second part, called an extension, that is tacked on by the program that created it. If you write a letter in Microsoft Word and call it Budget 2000 it gets saved as Budget 2000.doc, and if you save an Excel spreadsheet with the same name it gets saved as Budget 2000.xls.

Viewing extensions

File extensions are there so that Windows and other programs know which files belong to them, and there's no reason why you shouldn't know too. Windows hides the names from you in an attempt to be helpful, leaving you to work out what a file does by deciphering its icon, but if you're going to become a Windows expert you need to be able to see complete file names. Turn them on by double clicking My Computer on the Windows Desktop. On the View menu click Folder Options (Options in Windows 95), then select the View tab. You'll find a tick in a box next to 'Hide file extensions for known file types'. Simply clear the tick, then click 'Show all files' to tell Windows you want it to reveal hidden and system files. Click OK.

Finding files

Once you're familiar with the file extensions Windows uses, you can really put the Find feature on the Start menu to work. Want to find all your Word documents? Just type *.doc. The * stands for any name so even if you can't remember what you called a file, a

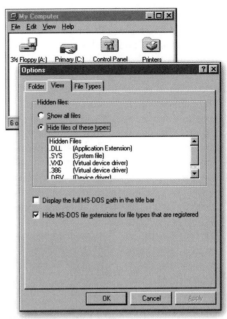

To turn on file extensions in Windows 95 double click My Computer, click View, then Options. Select the View tab in the Options box and clear the tick next to 'Hide MS-DOS file extensions for file types that are registered, also click 'Show all files.'

In Windows Me the Find feature on the Start menu has been renamed Search and given a makeover, but it works in much the same way as in Windows 95 and Windows 98.

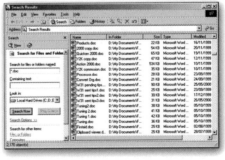

search for *.doc produces a list of all your Word documents, and if you know roughly when you created the file you can narrow the search still further using dates.

Setting up your graphics - step by step

The slowest element in any computer system is you, and regardless of how much you paid for your PC and how fast it's supposed to be you're the one that governs its speed. We've already looked at how to adjust the keyboard and mouse so they respond promptly to your commands. Now we're going to walk you through the even more important job of setting up your monitor. Do it properly and you'll be able to work or play for hours in front of your PC without any ill effects. Do it wrong – or don't do it at all – and you'll be in for headaches and sore eyes. You'll feel tired and get less done.

1 To determine the current set-up of your graphics system, which consists of a graphics card inside your computer to generate the picture and a monitor to display it, right click anywhere on the Windows Desktop and click Properties. In the Display Properties box click the Settings tab.

2 There are four key items of information on this screen: the number of colours being used, sixteen;

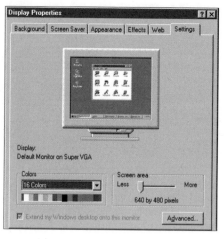

the screen area, 640 x 480; and the drivers controlling the monitor and graphics card, which in this case are drivers for a Default Monitor and a SuperVGA graphics card.

3 Default monitor and SuperVGA are very much bad news as far as performance is concerned. They're what Windows uses when it hasn't been able to work out the actual hardware in your PC. Ideally the monitor model should be shown and the graphics card should be named. If your graphics card is not named click the Advanced button, then the Adapter tab, otherwise skip to step 5.

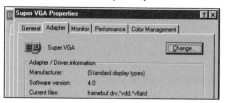

4 Click the Change button to Start the Update Device Driver Wizard. It will help you update your graphics card driver. You'll need to insert your Windows CD-ROM or the drivers supplied with the graphics card. Click Next, then select the recommended option to let Windows search for a better driver than the one you're using now. After Windows has restarted your computer repeat the above steps to view the effects.

Setting up your graphics (continued)

5 If the monitor is 'Plug and Play' Windows should be able to communicate with it and determine how best to use it. This isn't always the case, so if you were supplied with monitor drivers on disk or CD it's

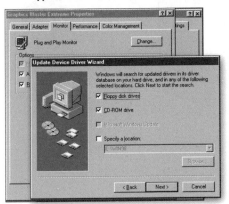

worth using them. To change drivers click the Monitor tab, then the Change button. Insert the driver disk, click Next and follow the instructions.

6 With the graphics card and monitor correctly identified it's time to choose how many colours to display and how big the screen area should be. For general use the optimum colour setting is usually High Color (16 bit). Most graphics cards are optimised for this setting and if yours is set to anything else, just click the Color box to change it.

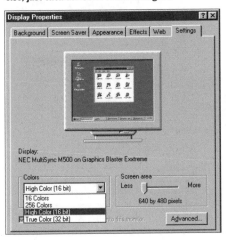

7 The Screen area slider controls how many dots are used to produce the picture on the screen, and the more dots you use, the more can be fitted onto the screen. The downside is that the dots are

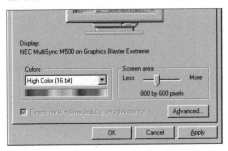

smaller so you shouldn't choose a screen area (or resolution to use the technical expression) that makes objects on the screen too small for comfortable viewing. As a guide, set 14in monitors to 640 x 480, 15in monitors to 800 x 600 and 17in monitors to 1024 x 768, then click Apply.

8 The final and most important setting to check is the refresh rate. In the Display Properties box click the Advanced button, then the Adapter tab. If the Refresh rate panel shows Optimal and you're not conscious of any screen flicker leave things alone. If the refresh rate is a number and it's 70Hz or lower, click to change it to 75Hz or above. Most experts recommend 75Hz or 85Hz to minimise eyestrain.

13

CHAPTER 2 **Desktop dealings**

With all the mundane preparations of the first chapter safely behind us it's time to have some fun. The Desktop is at the heart of Windows and is almost infinitely customisable. We can show you what's possible but how you arrange things is entirely up to you.

The ideal Desktop

With a big enough monitor you could have several Windows programs running at the same time and view them simultaneously on the Desktop. You'd then be able to switch between programs simply by clicking with the mouse on the appropriate window, and you could drag information from one program to another. With your address book open in one corner and your calculator in another you'd be able to work pretty much as you would with real objects on a real desk.

However big your monitor it always seems to be one size smaller than you really need, so it's important to make best use of the Desktop. One way of doing this is to maximise the

usable space by making the Taskbar at the bottom of the screen disappear when you're not using it. Just click with the right mouse button on an unused area of the Taskbar and when a menu pops up, click Properties. Tick the Auto hide option then click OK. Now, when you move the mouse cursor to the bottom of the screen the Taskbar appears. Move away and it disappears.

With a 17in monitor set to a resolution of 1024 × 768 and the Taskbar tucked out of sight you can comfortably run several programs and accessories.

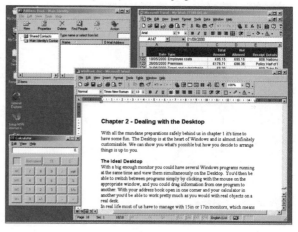

When you install a program into Windows it always adds itself to the menus on the Start button, and often you get an icon on the Desktop too. Strictly speaking you don't need both. Most people tend to stick to a single method of launching programs, usually via the Start menu, so the icon on the Desktop can be deleted to make more space. Simply right click an icon and select Delete to remove it.

Shortcuts

Note that by deleting an icon you're not deleting the program. The icon is simply a pointer to a program (it's actually called a shortcut) and when you click an icon it's like pointing at a program and saying, 'I want that one!'

As we said at the start of this chapter, it's up to you how you use the Desktop and maybe you actually like icons and want to have all your programs on the Desktop where you can see them. In Windows 98

Not everything on the Desktop can be deleted (the Recycle Bin for example) in which case the Delete option doesn't appear when you click the right mouse button. Here, with Outlook Express selected, deletion is possible.

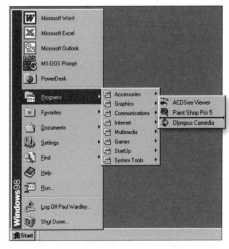

Holding down the mouse button on Paint Shop Pro, which is one of three programs in a group called Graphics, produces a separator line beneath it. Drag this line to where you'd like the program to go (even in another group) and then release the mouse button.

and Windows Me you can drag programs off the Start menu and drop them directly onto the Desktop.

Another convenient place to put your shortcuts is on the top level of the Start menu, where they appear above Programs. You'll notice there's a line at this point to separate your choice of programs from the built-in Windows options below. In Windows 98 and Windows Me you can drag a program from any sub-group of the Start button and drop it straight onto this top level for ease of access.

If you're a Windows 95 user and you're feeling left out of all this, it gets worse. Unlike its successors, Windows 95 doesn't have a Quick Launch area on the Taskbar. This is a block of easily-accessible icons next to the Start button. Windows 98 comes with three icons set up by default and Windows Me with four, but you can move programs into the Quick Launch area by dragging them from the Start menu or Desktop.

15

Making more of the Start Menu

As well as arranging programs on the Start menu so you can find them easily you can set things up so that every time you start Windows certain programs are loaded automatically. Some programs, when you install them, bind themselves into Windows so they run all the time – anti-virus programs are a good example – but any program can be made to start whenever Windows does by dragging its icon into the StartUp folder. You can access this by clicking Programs on the Start menu.

Obvious candidates for the StartUp folder are address books, diaries and personal organisers, but don't put the kitchen sink in there. Remember that the more programs there are in StartUp, the longer you'll have to wait for Windows to load.

Shrinking the Start menu

If you add too many programs to the top level of the Start menu, some of them disappear off the top of the screen and you have to click a little black triangle to scroll them back into view. This

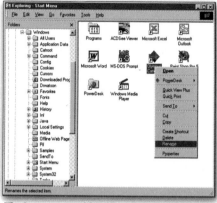

The Start menu is a folder like any other, and you can right-click any item inside it to rename or delete it.

negates the value of putting them there in the first place, which was for easy access. As long as you don't mind losing the Windows identification bar that runs up the side of the Start menu you can fit more programs onto it by reducing the size of the icons. Just right click a blank part of the Taskbar, click Properties, then put a tick in the box labelled 'Show small icons in Start menu.'

And did you know?

In Windows 98 and Windows Me you can rearrange the Start menu items from their standard alphabetical order into any order you like. Just drag them into position. You can't do this in Windows 95 but a neat alternative is to use Windows Explorer (on the Programs menu) to rename them. If you assign a number to each program the numbers will take priority over the alphabetical sort order. And, numbers make it easy to start programs without using the mouse. Just tap the Windows key to open the Start menu, tap the number and hit Enter.

Reducing the size of the icons on the Start menu reduces the size of the labels next to them and solves the problem of too many program shortcuts causing others to disappear off the top of the menu.

Variations on a theme

On the next page is our step-by-step guide
to setting up colours, backgrounds, fonts
and screen savers in any version of
Windows, but before you get your hands
dirty give a thought to using a Desktop
theme instead. These are not installed by
default but you can add them to Windows
98 and Windows Me using Windows Setup
as described on page 7. Themes were not
included with Windows 95 but were sold in
a separate Plus! Pack.

Installing Desktop Themes has no effect
until you choose one. This is done through
Control Panel, in which you'll find that a
new icon was added when Desktop Themes
were installed. Each theme offers co-ordi-
nating sounds, mouse pointers, wallpaper,
icons, colours, fonts and a screen saver. You
can either accept the entire package or
choose only the features you want by clearing some of the tick boxes on the right-hand
side of the selection screen. You may find
the more outlandish cursors and some of the
sound effects distracting.

Sound advice

The sound effects that accompany certain
Windows events, such as emptying the
Recycle Bin, can be changed by double-
clicking the Sound icon in Control Panel.
This opens the Sounds Properties box in
which you can highlight an item in the
Events panel, then pick a sound to go with
it from the panel below.

The sounds are ordinary Windows sound
files (with the extension .WAV), which you
can record for yourself using the Windows
Sound Recorder or download from many
sites on the internet. All you have to do is
store them in the Windows\Media folder
and they'll then appear in the list of sounds
you can assign to Windows events.

If you come up with a scheme you really
like but wouldn't want to use all the time
you can save it for future use by clicking the

Save As button and giving it a name. If, on
the other hand, you've gone overboard with
weird sounds and want to revert to the rela-
tive calm of the standard Windows sounds,
select Windows Default in the Schemes
panel of the Sounds Properties box.

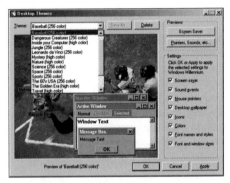

*The Baseball theme, like most others, works on any
PC but some themes require a high colour display setting and cannot be used on the 256-colour screens of
some older notebook and desktop PCs.*

*A customised sound scheme makes an unusual birth-
day present – or April Fool surprise – but make sure
you save the lucky user's standard scheme first!*

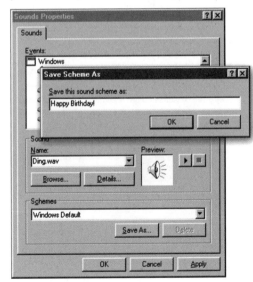

Customising your Desktop - step by step

Creating a personalised Desktop rather than using one of the predesigned themes is more likely to result in something you can live with on a permanent basis. Desktop themes may have a built-in wow factor but they're not necessarily designed to make Windows more usable, which is the real point of changing Desktop settings.

1 Changes to the appearance of the Desktop are made through the same Display Properties box we used in Chapter 1 to set up the graphics card and monitor. On that occasion we summoned the Display Properties box by right clicking on the Desktop and selecting Properties, but it's worth noting that you can also invoke it from within Control Panel by double clicking the Display icon.

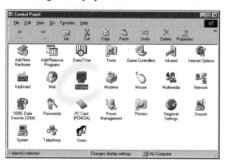

2 In Windows 98 and Windows Me there are six tabs across the top of the Display Properties box. Windows 95 lacks the Effects and Web tabs. Start with the Background tab and in the Wallpaper panel

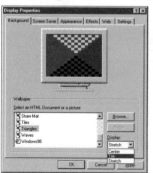

choose a picture to cover the plain blue-green Windows background. The picture will be previewed inside the Display Properties dialog box.

3 Small pictures can be stretched to fill the screen, as in step 2, or tiled so that they repeat until the screen is full. Larger pictures like this one from Windows Me should be centred. You can use your

own pictures by saving them in BMP format and putting them in the Windows folder (they'll appear in the list of wallpapers) or by selecting them from other folders after clicking the Browse button.

4 The Screen Saver tab is misleadingly named. Screen savers were originally designed to prevent static screen images becoming permanently etched into the phosphor of a monitor but now they're used for entertainment and relaxation. Choose one from the drop-down list for a miniature sample. Click Preview to view the effect full screen.

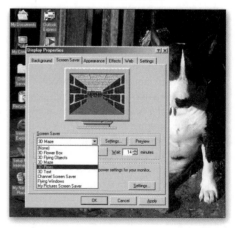

Customising your Desktop (continued)

5 The Settings button allows you to customise the way screen savers are drawn. The minutes specified in the Wait panel determine the period that must pass without any keyboard or mouse activity before the screen saver kicks in. Some screen savers provides a rudimentary form of password protection. With these, if you tick the Password Protected box, then click Change and type in a password, you can leave your PC unattended with the screen saver in action. Anybody trying to use your PC will be prompted for the password.

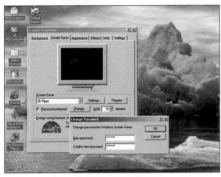

6 Also on the Screen Saver tab (we said it was misleadingly named!) are the options for power saving. These vary with each version of Windows and with the hardware inside each PC. In general there are three delay intervals to be set. These determine the period of inactivity required before the monitor

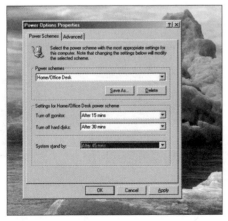

is turned off, hard disk activity is suspended and, finally, the entire PC is sent to sleep. Moving the mouse or pressing a key wakes it up again.

7 The Appearance tab isn't as complicated as it looks. It's where you change the colours, sizes and fonts of all the standard Windows buttons, labels, icons, borders etc. Simply click the item you want to

change in the upper half of the box, then select the options in the lower half. Click the Scheme panel to choose from a number of predefined combinations. Here we're changing the colour of the active title bar in the ready-made Pumpkin scheme.

8 Our last port of call (sorry, not for Windows 95 users) is the Effects tab. Of interest here are the five options in the Visual Effects panel. If you've got a slow PC, untick them all. You'll be amazed at the difference it makes. If your PC has power to spare try all the options. The most useful is Show Window

contents while dragging. It enables you to see exactly what a window looks like as you move or size it. With this option unticked all you see is a ghostly outline.

19

CHAPTER 3 Sharing a PC

Having a PC all to yourself solves a lot of problems. For example, you don't have to worry about someone else viewing your personal files or, even worse, deleting them. You can configure Windows to your own taste and make it work the way you want it to, either with a screen full of icons or a minimalist front end. Furthermore there's no doubt whose responsibility it is to maintain the PC and be responsible for preventive maintenance and troubleshooting. There are no arguments over which programs should be installed and, when using an internet connection, no compromises to make on passwords, security and email priorities.

In offices, one person to one computer is the norm, but at home it can be difficult to justify having a PC for every member of the family. Not only is it an expensive option, there's also the problem of where to put them all, especially if each has its own printer, speakers and accessories. In homes with two PCs (and the number of these is increasing as old computers are replaced with up-to-date

equipment) it's possible to have a 'serious' machine and one devoted to entertainment, but even this is only a partial solution because the files you need always tend to be on the other machine rather than the one that's free. Fortunately Windows includes several tools to ease the pain of sharing a PC, which we run through in this chapter, though if your real concern is making a PC safe for children to use on their own you may need to buy some additional software.

Having all this equipment to yourself is the ideal situation, but when you're forced to share it makes sense to tailor Windows accordingly.

By giving each user of a single PC a unique password it's possible for them to 'log on' when they start Windows and use a personalised Desktop scheme. Before setting up a PC in this way it's a good idea to have all the users agree who will be responsible for setting up passwords and making the necessary changes to the way Windows works. In a business environment this would be the system administrator. At home it

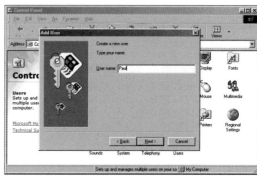

When you type a name into the Add User dialog box it can be anything you like – a first name, second name or nickname – but don't make it too complicated or unusual because you'll be typing it often.

might be Mum or Dad, but such is the way of the world it's just as likely to be a teenaged Jack or Jill.

On a typical Windows PC there's no need to log in – which means typing your name and a password – unless the computer is connected to other machines on a network, but when you want to share a single machine with other people you'll each need a password so that Windows can tell who's using the machine at any given time.

Creating the first user

To set up Windows 98 for multiple users you first set up the machine for yourself and then add as many other password identities as required. Start in Control Panel by double clicking the Users icon. This starts a Wizard that steps you through the process. Click Next to create the first user, which is yourself, and type your name. On the following screen enter your password twice, which is a simple check to make sure you've spelled it correctly. In common with most password entry screens all you'll see as you type is a row of asterisks. The final stage is to decide which aspects of Windows will be personalised for each user. There are five items and most people

decide to tick them all:

● Desktop and Documents folders (where the colours, icons, layout and wallpaper for the Windows Desktop and the locations of recently used files are stored)
● Start menu
● Favorites folder (mainly for your personal selection of frequently used Web pages)
● Downloaded Web pages
● My Documents folder (the folder where all your other documents are stored)

To make it easier to switch back to single user operation after having multiple users, you should select the option to 'Create copies of the current items and their content'.

Setting up multiple users (continued)

After the first user has been created Windows restarts and you have to type your name and password before Windows presents you with your personalised Desktop. At this stage everything will look the same as it always has because you're working with a copy of your old settings, but when you make changes to any of the five areas listed on page 21 they'll be recorded solely for your benefit.

Creating additional users

New users are added in the same way as you added yourself, by double clicking the User icon in Control Panel. The only difference is that you are first presented with a list

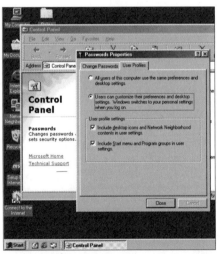

In the Password Properties dialog box when you select whether users will see their customised Desktops you may also choose whether they should have their own Start menus.

of the existing users so that instead of setting up a new identity you have the option of changing the settings for any of the existing users. To do so you'd need to know the password for every user whose settings you wanted to change, which is why we said at the outset that it's a good idea if one person

takes responsibility for setting up everybody's identity and keeps a log of the passwords and usernames.

Activating a multi-user system

When you set up a multi-user system on an older PC where others may have been tinkering in the past, you might find that Windows presents exactly the same settings to everybody regardless of which identity and password are typed. In this case open the Control Panel and double click the Passwords icon.

On the User Profiles tab you can choose whether all users should be presented with the same settings or whether personalised preferences should be used. Ensure that the correct option (Users can customise their preferences and Desktop settings...) has been selected.

Windows 95

In Windows 95 there is no Users icon with which you can add and maintain the details of multiple users in Control Panel. However, there is a Passwords icon on which you can click the User Profiles tab and then activate the multiple user feature as described above. Create new users by typing their names at the Windows opening screen. Passwords will need to be confirmed by entering them twice.

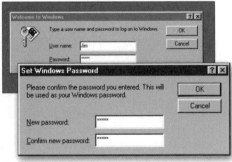

In Windows 95 new users are created by typing names at the opening screen rather than through the Windows Control Panel.

Sharing a computer means having house rules about leaving it in a fit state for others to use, and exactly the same goes for leaving Windows in a fit condition to use.

Drawbacks to user profiles

Setting up multiple user profiles is solely to allow users to personalise the look and feel of Windows. It does not provide security in the sense that it stops others viewing your files, using your programs or erasing material from the hard disk. In fact, anybody can log onto Windows without using a password simply by pressing the Escape key when presented with the log-on screen.

Agree a set of house rules

By far the best way of sharing a PC among family members and friends is to set up user profiles giving individuals the freedom to determine the look and feel of Windows, but each user should also agree to follow a simple set of house rules.

● No new software should be installed without the agreement of the other users (because installing new programs may have an impact on the existing ones by replacing Windows files or changing file associations).

● Nobody will change the default settings or options of Windows itself or any application program without the agreement of the others (so everyone knows what to expect).

● Each user will have an agreed maximum allocation of disk space (to prevent Windows slowing down if the hard disk becomes too full).

● Each user will keep all his/her documents in a single folder, though this may be split into as many sub-folders as necessary (to prevent confusion with duplicate file names).

● Nobody will move, delete or change the name of any file not in their own folder (in order to prevent the accidental deletion of other people's files).

To these essentials you can add your own stipulations regarding whether eating, drinking or smoking is allowed at the computer, who uses it when and who is responsible for cleaning it and backing it up.

Remember that user profiles and rules of etiquette are for convenience, not security. If you really want to protect your privacy and prevent unauthorised people from using your PC you will need to use software from a third party or alternatively some form of hardware locking device. A halfway house that costs nothing at all and provides enhanced (though not full) security for your PC is described on the next two pages.

23

System Policy Editor - step by step

The System Policy editor is provided in Windows 95 and Windows 98 for network administrators to control who does what on a network of computers. However, while ignoring most of the networking aspects, the owner of a standalone PC can use it to restrict the changes that sharers of a single PC are allowed to make. It offers a moderately high level of system security at zero cost.

1 Because of its specialised nature the System Policy Editor is not part of a typical Windows installation, nor is it even a conventional option. However, it can be installed from the Windows CD-ROM with the help of Windows Setup. Start this

in the usual way by double clicking the Add/Remove Programs icon in the Windows Control Panel, then click the Windows Setup tab followed by the Have Disk button.

2 In the Install from Disk dialog box click the Browse button and select your CD-ROM drive (E: in our screenshot). If you have Windows 95 click through the folders on the CD until you get to

admin\apptools\poledit. If you have Windows 98 the appropriate folder is tools\reskit\netadmin\poledit. When you've found the folder, click OK twice.

3 In the Have Disk dialog box tick System Policy Editor followed by the Install button. When the installation is complete (it takes only a few seconds) you can close the Add/Remove programs box and you'll find that System Policy Editor has been added to the System Tools group of Accessories on the Start menu.

4 The System Policy Editor makes changes to a single user profile at a time, so if you've set up more than one you should restart Windows and log on as the user whose rights you wish to restrict. Then start the System Policy Editor and click the File

Menu, on which you should select Open Registry. You'll be presented with two icons labelled Local User and Local Computer. Click Local User.

5 For Windows 95 users there are five broad areas of activity listed in the Local User Properties box. These are designated as Control Panel, Desktop, Network, Shell and System. Windows 98 users will

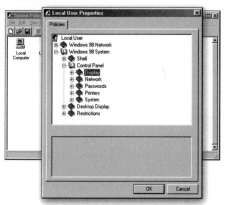

find Network Settings separated from the other four, which are grouped under Windows 98 System. When you double click any area of activity, further options are displayed, as shown here, where Control Panel has been opened.

6 Double click Display and you'll see what looks like a single option labelled Restrict Display Control Panel, but ticking this reveals further settings in the lower panel of the dialog box. By selecting these you can disable individual tabs on the Display Control Panel or all of them. Hide Settings page, as selected here, is useful because it prevents users setting a screen size beyond the capabilities of the monitor.

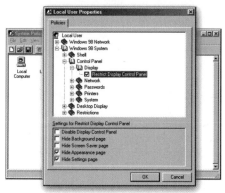

7 Many of the most useful settings are in the Shell group. If you open this up and take a look at the items listed under Restrictions you can make sweeping changes such as hid-ing all the icons on the

Desktop, hiding drives in My Computer (to prevent floppy disks and CD-ROMs being used) and even disabling the Shut Down command. To apply the changes you've made click OK, then choose Exit from the File menu and when you are asked if you want to save changes to the Registry, answer Yes.

8 The ultimate restriction you can impose, espe-cially if you're trying to control what children get up to on an unattended PC, is to completely block access to all programs except those you have specif-ically selected. THIS MUST BE DONE WITH EXTREME CAUTION. When compiling a list of per-mitted programs you must include the System Policy Editor itself (it's called Poledit.exe). If you don't, you'll never be able to change that user's pro-file again and the restrictions you make will remain permanently in force! The screen below shows that all programs apart from Excel (excel.exe), Word (winword.exe) and the System Policy Editor (poled-it.exe) have been forbidden.

CHAPTER 4

Getting connected

With the successes and failures of dotcom companies regularly making the national news headlines and practically every corner shop having its own web site, it comes as no surprise to most computer users that a PC linked to the internet has become as important a tool for communication as radio, TV and telephone.

Thanks is due in large part to Windows, which makes it easy for sound, pictures and text to be combined. Having said this,

Windows did not drive the communications revolution. Computers successfully exchanged messages and information for years before Windows was even thought of, but the point-and-click simplicity of Windows and the fact that Windows and the internet grew up together have made the two ideally suited.

Recent trends

Setting up computer communications used to be something of a black art. It meant using a special language full of strange expressions like stop bits, baud rates and transfer protocols. Even worse, you needed different communications programs for every type of computer you wanted to connect to. Many of these complexities are still there but they're handled in the background by Windows and the companies providing internet services.

The two main Windows communications tools – Internet Explorer and Outlook Express – also serve to hide many of the behind-the-scenes complexities, but if you're prepared to delve just a little way behind their friendly facades and learn something about how they can be configured to work more effectively you'll be able to make Windows communicate even more effectively for business and recreation.

With home banking, home shopping and online holiday bookings rapidly becoming the norm you might lose out by ignoring the communications revolution.

Apart from the PC itself there are three requirements for using the internet: a modem, a telephone line and an internet service provider. The modem is a go-between that turns signals from a PC into something that can be transmitted along a phone line. New PCs are sold with one already inside them, or you can buy a modem that slots inside an older machine. If you don't want to open up your computer you can go for an external unit that plugs into a serial port on the back of your PC.

Whether your modem is an internal or external type, before you can use it you'll have to connect it to a standard phone socket using the cable provided. It's OK to use an adapter so that your telephone handset and the modem can be connected to the same socket but you can't make a voice call and use your modem at the same time.

Service providers

Internet service providers (ISPs) are companies that own and maintain computers connected to the internet. They give you a telephone number which you can use to connect your PC via the phone line to their computers. Some of them charge for this service, others provide it free and make a charge for help calls. Free providers might bombard you with unsolicited information and, of course, you can hardly complain if the service is slow or their computer is permanently engaged when you're not paying for it.

Service providers advertise in newspapers and computer magazines. Some of them give away introductory CD-ROMs with other products and you may have seen these on offer in book and record shops as well as computer stores. Another way of getting connected is to start the Internet Connection Wizard that's built into Windows. This will call a referral service and is supposed to offer a choice of ISPs for your area, though when we tried it with an

The CD-ROMs supplied by internet service providers do everything for you in terms of setting up Windows communication features, but you'll have to supply personal details and, perhaps, a credit card number.

early version of Windows Me it came up only with Virgin.net. Whichever service you choose you will end up with an internet account that's ready to use for sending and receiving email, and for surfing the web.

Windows' Internet Connection Wizard can be started from the Welcome to Windows introduction or by clicking Connect to the Internet on the Desktop. It will also start if you attempt to run a communications program such as Internet Explorer without an internet connection.

Setting internet options 1

Internet Explorer is continually revised and improved. Depending on which version of Windows you have – and whether you've recently used Microsoft's Windows Update facility – you could have anything from version 3 to version 5.5, which is the one supplied with Windows Me. To find out which one you're using you should start Internet Explorer and click About Internet Explorer on the Help menu. The information here relates to version 5, which is the one most people have, but similar facilities exist in other releases.

AltaVista is a popular search engine to use as a home page, especially in its UK-specific form. Here we've pressed F11 to strip away the usual Windows clutter.

The Google search engine has been chosen as home page by clicking the Use Current button. This is a much more reliable method than typing an address.

Getting the big picture

Good web sites are designed to be viewed on any PC, regardless of what screen resolution is being used, but most of them are best viewed at 800 × 600 or 1024 × 768. If you customarily have Windows set at 640 × 480 you'll get along much better with Internet Explorer by temporarily switching to 800 × 600 before connecting to the internet (see page 13).

Whatever resolution you're using you can maximise the amount of visible information by using F11 (that's the function key on the top row of the keyboard) which strips away the usual Windows title, menu and frame to provide a full-screen view with a single control bar across the top. Just press F11 again to revert to a standard display.

General settings

On the Tools menu of Internet Explorer you will find Internet Options. This is to Internet Explorer what the Control Panel is to Windows itself. Every aspect of how your PC will connect to the internet can be modified from here. There are six tabbed sections of options, the obvious starting point being the General tab on the left. Most people want to set the home page, which is the first page you see when connecting to the internet, to something other than Microsoft or an internet service provider. If you've got a web page of your own you might use this, but many people choose to have their favourite search engine as their home page. The easiest way of setting the home page is to visit it and then, while it's on-screen, start Internet Options and click Use Current on the General tab.

28

The two other main options on the General tab concern how and where temporary internet files are stored, and how long the history of pages you've visited is remembered by your PC. Both of these can be changed but the default settings tend to work for most people.

Of the four buttons along the bottom, Colors and Fonts are the two worth looking at if you want to change the general appearance of web pages, but the choices you make on these buttons only apply when the designer of a web page has failed to specify alternatives.

Security zones

One of the concerns of internet users is that when visiting certain web sites potentially harmful programs and other code might be downloaded to their PCs. The sorts of things to be wary of are ActiveX controls (in effect, small programs that load themselves onto your PC and run from within Internet Explorer) and cookies, which are the coded

If you use the internet purely for recreational purposes, you're more likely to reduce security than increase it – this results in fewer questions and interruptions, but you have to feel happy about unrestricted information flowing into your PC.

calling cards your PC collects from sites you have visited. Cookies are used to store information about you, including viewing preferences and membership information for sites that require you to sign in. The worry is that your cookies might be analysed by a rogue site in an attempt to build up a picture of you and your browsing habits.

On the Security tab of Internet Options you can set different levels of security for four internet zones. One of these, Local intranet, won't concern you unless you're part of a company network. Two of the other zones are Trusted sites (Microsoft, BBC, Inland Revenue etc) and Restricted sites (usually these sites have names along the lines of PirateProgs.com and MoneyforNothing.co.uk). Every site that's not listed as trusted or restricted belongs to the main zone called simply Internet.

The default security settings are high for restricted sites, low for trusted sites and medium for all other sites on the internet. The settings can be changed simply by moving a slider control. If, because you have particularly sensitive information on your PC or you are in any way worried about security and you'd like more protection, you can increase it, but take note that some sites will not work at a high security setting which forbids the cookies on which some sites depend.

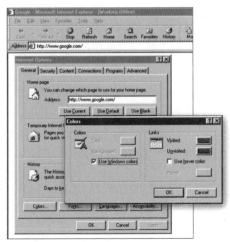

When Use Windows colors is ticked, web pages without their own colour scheme will use the same font colours as Windows (usually black on white) but if you untick this option you can choose a special scheme specifically for web pages.

For adults only

Parents who are concerned that their children might view unsuitable or adult material on the web can use the Content tab to make

The default settings for sites rated by the Recreational Software Advisory Council (RSACi) are certain not to offend anyone, but you may decide to relax the rules slightly by moving slider controls to the right.

that have no rating' is unticked. With these settings in place, the only sites that may be viewed are those rated as suitable by the Recreational Software Advisory Council and those you type in yourself on the Approved Sites tab. If you feel this form of control is too restrictive or inflexible, you'll need to invest in a Third Party program such as Cyber Patrol or Net Nanny, which are almost infinitely configurable.

Personal profiles save typing

While you're on the Settings tab you might like to set up a personal profile. This stores information about you which can be passed automatically to sites that require on-screen forms to be completed. To input your details click the My Profile button. When the Windows Address book pops up click OK and then fill in only those details you're prepared to make known.

It's not usual to store your own details in an address book but that's where Internet Explorer looks for a personal profile.

certain sites unviewable. Those armed with a password can turn the restrictions off. To set the password click the Enable button in Content Advisor. Once this has been done click the Settings button and use the Ratings slider controls to set the levels of language, nudity, sex and violence you feel are appropriate. Then click the General tab and look in the User options panel. Make sure that the box labelled 'Users can see sites

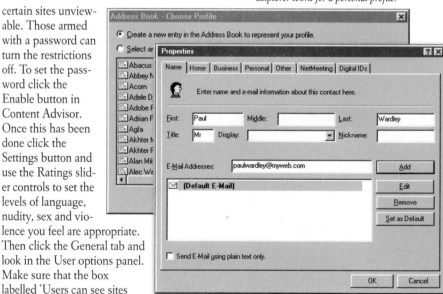

Internet Explorer partner programs

Internet Explorer handles every kind of web-related activity but it can't be used to send and receive email or to participate in newsgroups. What it can and does do is tie in closely with another Windows program called Outlook Express, which is able to handle email and newsgroups. Outlook Express is the default program for both these functions but if you'd rather use an alternative program for email (which would be the case if you had Microsoft Outlook or another personal information manager) you can choose the preferred software from the drop-down list on the Internet options Programs tab. The email and news programs you choose here will be started by Internet Explorer whenever you select Read Mail or Read News on the Tools menu.

Faxing from Windows

These days it's impossible to buy a modem that isn't able to send and receive faxes but Microsoft seems to be shying away from faxing in favour of basing all communications

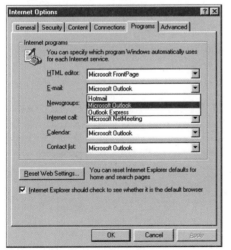

When you install a program with a communications component, such as an email handler, it should be automatically added to the drop-down lists on the Programs tab. If it isn't, you won't be able to start it from within Internet Explorer.

on the internet. Windows 95 users can install Microsoft Fax from the Add/Remove Programs tool in Control Panel but this is not the case with Windows 98 or Me. You must use a third-party fax program. One is usually supplied with a modem, though it's often a 'Lite' version of a program with more extensive capabilities.

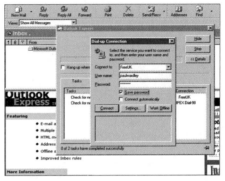

The first time you use email you'll be asked to type in your password. If at the same time you tick the Save password box you'll never be asked this question again, but by doing so you're allowing anybody else who uses your PC to read your mail.

If you're a Microsoft Office user or have the full version of Outlook (not Outlook Express) you have access to Symantec Winfax Starter Edition, which you can install from the program CD. This can be used from within Outlook, in which faxes are treated just like email messages because they arrive in your Inbox and are despatched from the Outbox. You'll also be able to send faxes from other programs by going through the motions of printing them but selecting Symantec Fax Starter Edition instead of your usual printer.

One thing to check when sending a fax is that it may be a two-stage process, depending which fax program you use and how you go about it. You may find that a fax is not sent immediately but stored in the Outbox of your communications program for transmission along with your email.

Setting up newsgroups - step by step

Newsgroups are public forums where you can leave messages for others to read, and you can read the messages other members of the group have left. While email is the electronic equivalent of sending a letter, posting a message to a newsgroup is like writing to the letters page of a newspaper. If there's a difference it's that newsgroups tend to focus on very narrow subjects such as pet welfare, stamp collecting and time travel rather than topics of universal interest.

Though most ISPs provide newsgroup services it's not often that they're set up for you automatically in the same way as email accounts. On these pages we step you through setting up and using newsgroups.

1 You'll need to contact your ISP to find out the name of its news server. This will be something like news.dial.pipex.com, which is the news server for Pipex Dial. If your ISP provides answers to frequently asked questions (FAQs) on its web pages you'll probably find the name of the news server there. Once you've got it, connect to the internet and start Outlook Express, then click Accounts on the Tools menu.

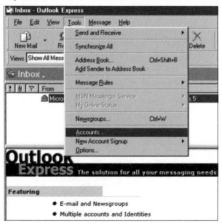

2 In the Internet Accounts dialog box click the Add button to choose News from the three types of account available. The others are Mail and Directory service. The Internet Connection Wizard will then

prompt you for the name you wish to use in Newsgroups, which may be your real one or a nickname. When you've typed it, click Next.

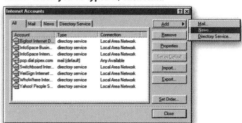

3 When you're asked to type your email address, which is what readers will use to respond to your newsgroups messages, it's a good idea to disguise it

by inserting some dummy material in brackets. Anybody reading an email address like paulwardley@[remove this]dial.pipex.com will know that they have to remove the bracketed part. It's a precaution is to stop your name being 'harvested' by automatic programs that will bombard you with junk mail.

4 The Wizard will prompt you for the name of the news server. When you've given this and clicked Finish you can accept the offer to have the list of newsgroups downloaded from the server you've just added.

Setting up and using newsgroups (continued)

When you download the list of groups from a news server you don't get any messages, just the names of the groups. There are more than 30,000 of these, the number changing daily as they come and go.

5 With a news account established you can participate in newsgroups by switching to Outlook Express from within Internet Explorer. To do so click the Mail

button on the Explorer toolbar and select the Read News option. When Outlook Express has loaded, select Newsgroups from the Tools menu. If you get a message announcing that you are not subscribed to any newsgroups and offering to display a list of them, click Yes.

6 Either scroll through the list to find a group that sounds interesting or type a search word in the top panel, such as 'mini'. A list of all the groups containing 'mini' in their names will be displayed. If you're interested in cars, not MINIstries or DoMINIon, select alt.autos.mini and click the 'Go to' button. This downloads the most recent 300 messages in

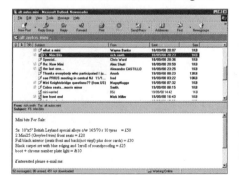

the group. To see more you click 'Get next 300 headers' on the Tools menu. What you get are header lines, not complete messages. To view a message, click its header line and the message is displayed in the lower panel.

7 Reply to a message by right-clicking its header. If you choose Reply to Group your message will appear for others to read. If you choose Reply to Sender it's just like sending an ordinary email to one person.

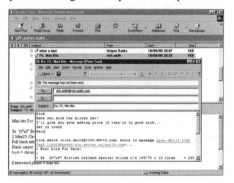

8 Instead of using the 'Go to' button to view a newsgroup, as in step 6, you can double click the name of the group to subscribe to it (free of charge). The newsgroups you subscribe to are listed automatically when Outlook Express starts. This saves searching through 30,000 groups for the ones of interest, and a bonus is that if you tick the box to the right of the newsgroup's listing you'll then be able to click the Synchronise Account button and download only the new messages in the group when you next log on.

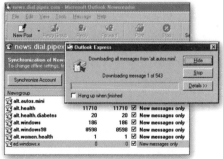

CHAPTER 5 Multimedia basics

the Windows wave format, synthesised music in Midi format and video clips in the relatively low-quality Windows audiovisual interleave format. The three types of file can be recognised by the three-letter WAV, MID or AVI extensions to their file names (assuming you've turned these on, as described on page II).

When these are combined with imaginative graphics and illustrations, cartoon-style animations and high resolution photographs the overall effect can be quite dazzling on even an ordinary PC equipped with a standard sound card and small desktop speakers.

Anybody old enough to remember the Sixties will recall over-hyped multimedia shows relying on little more than coloured lights and slide projectors backed by a soundtrack. We've moved on a great deal since then to laser lighting, holograms and Dolby surround sound, but as far as Windows is concerned multimedia is still the straightforward combining of sounds, pictures and words.

What you need

Whereas you once paid extra for multimedia, the features you need are now standard on all new PCs. Basically these are a sound card, speakers and a CD-ROM drive able to handle the massive files required for video and music clips. Everything you need for audiovisual playback is built into Windows but the tools for creating multimedia are limited, so anybody with a professional interest in the subject will need additional third-party software.

What you can do

Most CD-ROM encyclopaedias incorporate all the standard Windows multimedia features: recorded sounds (speech and music) in

Microsoft Encarta manages to deliver all its multimedia content using only the features built into Windows. Other encyclopaedias may install additional software such as Apple's QuickTime video player.

Making your own multimedia

Though Windows is adept at playing many kinds of multimedia files, the only multimedia files you can make for yourself using Windows 95 or 98 are wave (WAV) files. These might be live recordings made using a microphone or prerecorded material from a sound source connected to the line-in socket of the sound card.

Windows 95 plays video files in the AVI and MPG formats through a simple player called ActiveMovie.

To record a Midi file you need a Midi sound source, such as a digital musical instrument connected to the sound card, plus additional recording software. Having said this, some sound cards are bundled with a simple Midi recording tools and an on-screen digital keyboard that you can 'play' with your mouse if all you want to do is experiment.

Windows Me

The situation is rather different in Windows Me. Microsoft has introduced a new format called Windows Media, in which WMA (Windows Media Audio) and WMV (Windows Media Video) seem set to replace the old WAV and AVI formats. Another innovation

is that Windows Me includes a program called Windows Movie Maker, with which you can edit and save movies using clips downloaded from digital video cameras. These can be combined with still pictures, backing tracks and an audio overdub.

All multimedia formats in Windows Me are played by the new version 7 of Windows Media Player, which is also downloadable as an upgrade for Windows 98. It not only replaces the old Windows CD Player but also incorporates a CD recorder that converts CD audio tracks into the new WMA format and saves them on hard disk for subsequent playback on a PC or a suitable portable audio player.

In one sense WMA is trying to steal the market that has already been grabbed my MP3. As music lovers will be aware, this is a highly compressed way of storing high-quality music files for use by portable audio players. WMA and MP3 are not compatible, they're two different ways of doing the same thing and it remains to be seen whether hybrid players able to use both types of file will emerge or whether we'll see a VHS/Beta-style shootout.

Media Player 7, as supplied with Windows Me, plays all the old Windows sound and video formats as well as some new ones. In addition you get picture controls and sound adjustment just like a real TV.

Changing multimedia settings

The default settings for how Windows handles multimedia don't usually need changing if all you're going to do is play prerecorded files, but if you've got an advanced sound system with multiple speakers or are planning on recording your own audio it's worth opening up Control Panel and double clicking the Multimedia icon to see if the standard settings are making the most of your equipment.

Speaker settings

On the Audio tab of Multimedia Properties in Windows 98 are two panels labelled Playback and Recording, each with its own button for advanced settings. In the Playback panel the name of the sound card is displayed as the preferred device. Never change this unless you have two different sound cards in one PC.

Clicking Advanced Properties in Playback displays a secondary dialog box. Its two tabs are labelled Speakers and Performance. On the Speakers tab is a drop-down list from which you can select the type of speakers connected to your PC – anything from a simple headset to a five-speaker surround sound system – and thus make Windows generate the optimum output for your speakers. It's well worth changing this to match your hardware.

Audio performance

On the Performance tab are two slider controls. The Hardware Acceleration slider should be set to full and there's no reason to change it unless sound output is suffering from unexplained clicks or periods of silence. The other slider control determines the playback quality of digitised sound files and is best left at its lowest (Good) setting for general purposes and games, though you might move it to Better or Best if your primary interest is mixing and editing CD-quality audio files.

The Advanced Properties button on the Recording panel displays the same two sliders as in the Playback panel and the same strictures apply. The only other option you might consider changing is whether the volume control should appear on the taskbar of the Windows Desktop. Normally this is a useful facility but if your sound card has added its own icon you might want to remove the Windows one by clearing the tick on the Audio tab.

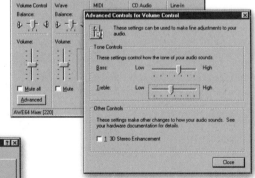

If you click the loudspeaker icon on the taskbar a simple volume control pops up, but did you know that you double click the icon to get at your sound card's mixer control? The Advanced button on the mixer may lead to further goodies, depending on the features of the sound card in your machine.

A surround sound speaker system involves five speakers, including one facing directly towards you. If you have two pairs of speakers, front and back, select Quadraphonic Speakers.

CD-ROM and DVD drives

If you've recently bought a new PC it's likely to be fitted with a DVD drive as well as a CD-ROM drive unless it's a bargain-basement machine. Even then you could always fit one as an upgrade. This couldn't be easier if you're replacing an existing CD-ROM drive with a DVD drive; you just remove the old unit and connect the new one to the same cables.

Installing a DVD drive alongside an existing CD-ROM drive isn't much trickier. They can share the same data cable; it's just a question of setting switches on the back of one of the drives so that Windows knows which is which. One must be set as a master and the other as a slave.

Playing DVD movies

As far as Windows is concerned a DVD drive is just another type of CD-ROM drive and it can used be for exactly the same purposes, installing and running software and playing audio CDs. The other use for DVD drives is, of course, playing movies. You can't fit two hours' of high quality audio and video onto an ordinary CD, and this is one of the main reasons why DVD was invented.

The movies on DVD drives are coded and to play them you need a decoder. This

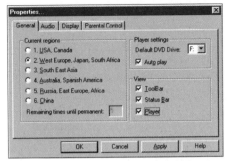

Regional settings have nothing to do with the languages spoken in DVD movies. Many movies come with soundtracks and captions in several languages. Regional coding is a deterrent to software piracy.

can be a hardware device fitted inside your PC or a software decoder devoted to playing DVD movies. In many respects software decoding is a better option than hardware because it's cheaper and can be upgraded more easily, but smooth software decoding requires a moderately fast PC – certainly nothing slower than a 350MHz Celeron or its AMD equivalent.

Without a hardware or software decoder you can't play DVD movies, and it's rather surprising that Microsoft has not built DVD playback into Windows Me. The reason may be related to copyright issues. DVD movies are produced in six versions according to the region of the world in which they're to be sold (region 2 for the UK). It's important to buy movies for your own region. Although you can change the regional setting of a DVD drive up to five times, it then becomes permanently locked.

WinDVD 2000 is one of several popular software decoders for DVD movies. Even software decoders have to be paid for so if you're buying a DVD drive it's worth looking for one that's bundled with a player. Failing this it's worth checking to see if one is included with your graphics card drivers.

Configuring CD and DVD drives - step by step

In one sense you don't need to do anything to your CD-ROM or DVD drives – they just work – and you can leave Windows to get on with them. But if you take this position you'll miss out on some of their potential so here, in step-by-step form, is how to set up your drives most effectively.

1 On the Windows Desktop, right click on My Computer and select Properties. In the System Properties dialog box click the Device Manager tab,

then double click the entry labelled CDROM. In our example there are two devices, one Creative and one Ricoh. Neither of them is a standard CD-ROM drive, one being DVD and the other CD-Rewritable, but this doesn't matter to Windows, which treats them both as CD-ROM drives.

2 Double click the entry for your CD-ROM drive, or the first drive if you have more than one. This displays its properties. Click the Settings tab. The

tick in the box labelled Auto insert notification means that when you insert a disc in the drive it plays automatically. You may have noticed this happening with both data CD-ROMs and audio CDs. It's actually very annoying when you're just trying to load a sample file from a CD-ROM so you may wish to remove the tick to disable this feature.

3 On the same tab there's a box labelled DMA, which stands for Direct Memory Access. Placing a tick next to it tells Windows to access the CD-ROM directly, wasting less of the processor's time. Not all CD-ROM drives can use DMA and even if you get a message like the one shown below, there's no harm in trying. Click OK and restart your PC.

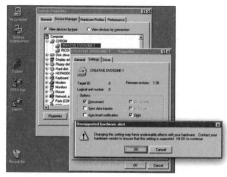

4 If you have two drives there may be one you'd rather use for playing audio CDs, perhaps because it's faster than its partner or because the other is used for recording. In this case you can tell Windows which drive to use for playing audio CDs by opening the Multimedia Properties box, as described on page 36, and clicking the CD Music tab. From the drop-down list pick the drive you want to use for music CDs and click OK.

Configuring CD and DVD drives (continued)

Though there's little point in using a PC to play audio CDs if it's in the same room as a domestic music centre, there are very good reasons for playing audio CDs on a PC in other circumstances. For one thing many PCs now have better sound output than cheap music centres, and being able to control the volume from your PC means you don't have to leap across the room if the phone rings.

5 If the drive you're using to play audio CDs has auto insert notification turned on all you have to do is insert a disc in the drive and CD Player will start playing it. The only visual indication of what's happening is that track and time information is displayed on the Windows taskbar.

6 To see the Windows CD Player in all its glory click the indicator on the taskbar. Alternatively, if autoplay is not enabled you can start CD Player manually by tracking it down on the Start menu. It's buried away in either an Entertainment or Multimedia folder within the Accessories group.

7 CD Player sports the familiar playback control buttons. In addition, on the Options menu there is Random Play (the same as Shuffle play on a standard CD deck) and the very useful Intro Play, which plays the first ten seconds of each track for identification purposes. On the View menu you can choose between three different time displays.

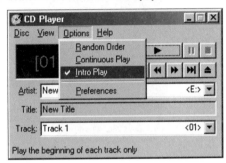

8 The most useful feature of all, if you have the patience to set it up, is on the Disc menu and is called Edit Play List. Here you can enter the artist and disc title at the top, and in the panel at the bottom identify all the individual tracks by typing a name and clicking Set Name for each one. Any or all of the tracks on a disc can be added to the play list in any order by selecting each track in turn and clicking the Add button. The clever part, though, is that Windows recalls this information the next time you insert the disc and knows which tracks to play and what they're called.

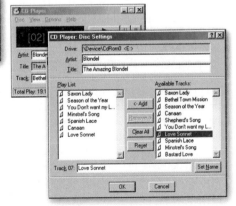

CHAPTER 6

Tuning up your PC

Tuning Windows has two main outcomes: speed and reliability. The speed of Windows is not judged by how fast you can calculate a spreadsheet or check the spelling of a document, it's more a question of how smoothly Windows can be made to respond to your commands and of minimising the wait for things to start happening.

Objective speed tests can be implemented, and they're useful to magazine reviewers when comparing several machines, but they're of limited use to PC owners because everybody uses a PC differently, and the well-tuned machine for playing games is very different from the well-tuned business PC.

Reliability is linked to efficiency, and many of the tuning techniques for increasing speed, such as eliminating fragmented and unnecessary files on a hard disk, also lead to greater reliability. In essence, the aim of tuning is to strip out the extra baggage that Windows accumulates over time and try to return it to the lean and mean state it was in when first installed. Once this has been done it's a relatively straightforward operation to tweak all the adjustable Windows settings to suit the way you work.

Take stock

Before doing anything remotely technical take stock of your PC and the programs on it. Do you actually use all those programs or are some of them there simply because they were preinstalled when you bought the machine? Anything you don't use should be ruthlessly chopped to create more disk space and reduce the jumble of files.

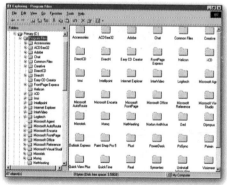

To track down all the programs installed on your PC use a three-pronged approach. First scan the entries on the Start menu, then view the list of programs in the Add/Remove programs dialog box. Finally, find any you may have missed by using Windows Explorer to browse the Program Files folder, as shown here.

When removing a program don't simply delete its files and folders, make sure you remove it completely through the Add/Remove programs feature in Control Panel. Many programs when they're first installed do far more than copy themselves into a new folder; they modify existing Windows settings and may even replace certain Windows files with new versions. Using Add/Remove Programs will try to undo these changes as well as deleting the program's own files and folders. Only when you've 'officially' removed a program should you manually delete any traces that may be left, such as stray files and empty folders.

Disk Cleanup

Disk Cleanup is a Windows 98 program designed to trim unneeded files, mainly temporary ones generated while using the internet and by business software such as word processors, spreadsheets and accounting programs. You'll find Disk Cleanup on the Start button if you click Programs, then

select Accessories followed by System Tools.

In the opening panel of Disk Cleanup select the drive you wish to clean, which if you have only one hard disk will be C:, then click OK. The selected disk will be scanned for surplus files and these are presented in a dialog box that categorises them as temporary internet files, downloaded program files, offline web pages, the contents of the Recycle bin or any other temporary files not included in the above.

Deleting temporary internet files saves space but may slow down internet browsing in the short term because it deletes the pages you use regularly as well the ones you'll never visit again. Fortunately it doesn't take long to rebuild a store of regularly visited pages. It's usually safe to delete all the downloaded program files because if you needed them permanently you'd have stored them elsewhere on disk after downloading them, but whether or not you should delete the web pages saved for offline reading depends whether you finished reading them. If you're not sure what they are, highlight Offline Web Pages and click the View Pages button. Unfortunately while viewing them you can't select individual pages for deletion. It's all or nothing.

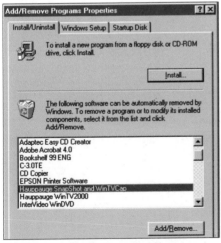

To delete a program and all its related files open Control Panel and double click Add/Remove programs. On the Install/Uninstall tab select a program and then click Add/Remove. Some programs can't be fully removed until Windows has been restarted.

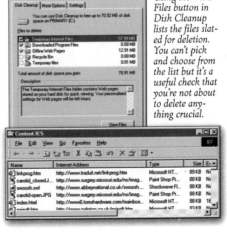

Using the View Files button in Disk Cleanup lists the files slated for deletion. You can't pick and choose from the list but it's a useful check that you're not about to delete anything crucial.

Close up disk gaps

Deleting the contents of the Recycle Bin from within Disk Cleanup has exactly the same effect as emptying the bin on the Desktop after right clicking it. Anything in the bin is permanently erased, which releases disk space but makes it impossible to recover items from the bin if you later change your mind.

The remaining files handled by Disk Cleanup are those created by Windows and other programs as temporary workspace. These are meant to be cleared away automatically by programs as they close; all Disk Cleanup does is round up the stragglers. When you've ticked which categories of files you'd like to delete click OK. The rest is automatic. Disk Cleanup is not included with Windows 95 but you can delete temporary internet files by using Internet Options on the Tools menu of Internet Explorer, as described on page 29.

Defragmentation

Every time a scrap of information is deleted from a hard disk it leaves a space. When there are more spaces than files, the magnetic head of a hard disk has to swing madly back and forth between the gaps looking for data. A disk with lots of spaces is said to be fragmented, and defragmenting it simply means getting rid of the spaces and moving all the files into a single block.

Nothing you can do to your PC does it more good than defragmenting the disk, after which it starts faster and runs more smoothly. Obviously, if you've just deleted excess baggage from a disk by removing unwanted programs and using Disk Cleanup as described above there'll be

more spaces on it than ever, which is why disk defragmentation should always go hand in hand with a clean up.

The program that does the work for you is called Disk Defragmenter, and it's on the System Tools menu along with Disk Cleanup. When it starts, first select the drive you want to defragment from the drop-down list, then click the Settings button. Tick both option boxes. One confirms that you'd like programs rearranged to make your PC start faster, and the other makes sure the drive is checked for errors.

The option to have programs rearranged to make a PC start faster is available only in Windows 98. Although Disk Defragmenter in Windows 95 lacks this feature it's still worth using it to close up the gaps between data.

Disk Defragmenter works unattended and may take many hours to do its work. If you want to see what it's doing click the Show Details button after starting it.

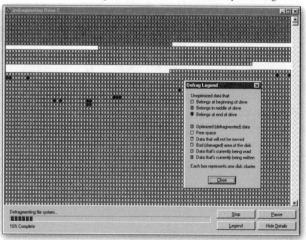

Disk defragmentation takes time, often many hours, so the best time to run it is overnight. You can't run it while you're working at your PC because Disk Defragmenter restarts every time another program changes the contents of the hard disk.

To make it easier to run Disk Cleanup and Disk Defragmenter at odd hours or when the PC is unattended, Windows 98 includes Maintenance Wizard. This is a tool that runs Disk Cleanup and Disk Defragmenter at scheduled intervals. It has no equivalent in Windows 95.

Start it by clicking Maintenance Wizard on the System Tools menu. It has two options, Express and Custom. In Express mode the program checks the hard disk, deletes all unnecessary files and defragments the hard disk at the times you specify. You may prefer to specify your own settings in Custom mode. You are then able to specify which hard disks get defragmented (if your machine has more than one) and you may also choose which files to delete during the clean-up process. You might decide, for example, to have the Maintenance Wizard delete your temporary internet files but keep your offline web pages intact until you decide you've finished with them.

Task scheduler

After setting up the Maintenance Wizard you'll notice an icon on the right of the taskbar which may not have been there before. It's the Windows Task Scheduler. If you right click it and select Open you'll see the individual tasks that have been scheduled by the Maintenance Wizard. From now on Task Scheduler will load every time you start Windows. If you disable it, the Maintenance Wizard will not perform its assigned tasks.

If you have other programs you want to automate you can assign them to the Task Scheduler by double clicking Add Scheduled Task. None of the built-in Windows programs are obvious candidates for scheduling but you might like to automate something like a virus checker if you have one from a third party. Simply pick the program from a list, or browse to it on the hard disk, and you'll then be prompted to choose when you'd like it to be run.

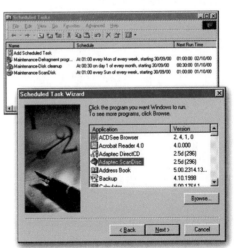

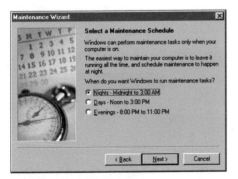

Choosing the Express option in Maintenance Wizard means the only decision you have to make is when to run the automatically allocated tasks. You'll need to leave your PC turned on, of course.

Adding a new program to the Task Scheduler is pretty straightforward but there's not much point in doing so unless the program you add is able to run completely unattended. Indexing programs that catalogue all the files on a disk (and sometimes take hours to run) are prime candidates for Task Scheduler.

Updating drivers

Your next task is to check that you've got the latest versions of all the Windows and third party drivers your PC requires. Drivers are the glue binding together the hardware and software components of your PC. Some are on the Windows installation CD-ROM and more are provided by the makers of the various components used by your PC.

You need them for, amongst other things, the sound card, modem and graphics cards inside your computer and the printer plugged into the back. Drivers handle the communications between Windows and each piece of hardware, so when Windows asks the sound card to produce a particular effect, it's the driver that tells the sound card how to do it. The advantage of using a driver is that if Microsoft changes something in Windows, or if the manufacturer of a component finds a better way of making it work, all that has to be changed is the driver, not the component.

Identifying drivers

Drivers are constantly improved, sometimes marginally and sometimes drastically. If you fail to update a driver that has been rewritten to fix a small bug or glitch it doesn't really matter, but missing a major update containing new features is a mistake.

No company is keen to send out driver updates on floppy disks or CD-ROMs and few of them will bother to write and tell you that there are new drivers available for your equipment. Having said this, manufacturers take drivers very seriously and produce frequent updates. The place to find out about them, and download them, is from the websites of equipment manufacturers. Identify new drivers by looking for the version number. Drivers, like programs, usually start at version 1.0. A driver numbered 1.01 will contain minor changes while 1.1 or 1.2 would be significantly improved. The introduction of a new driver

number like 2.0 or 3.0 would indicate a 'must have' upgrade. Updated files and drivers for Windows 98 and Windows Me can be obtained by using the Windows Update button on the Start menu. After logging onto the Microsoft site you'll be advised what's available.

In Windows 98 and Windows Me you'll find Windows Update on the Start menu. If you're a Windows 95 user, log onto the Microsoft website at www.microsoft.com and click Downloads instead.

Creative Labs, who make and supply a wide range of sound cards and multimedia components for your computer, make it easy to find the latest drivers with a search engine devoted to the task.

There are many settings within Windows related to improving performance. Some of them seem to make no difference however you set them, but cumulatively these minor adjustments do speed things up, as well as leading to increased reliability.

System performance settings

A tab to adjust system performance can be found in the System Properties dialog box. Start this from within Control Panel or use the shortcut, which is to right click My Computer on the Desktop and select Properties. Click the Performance tab and at the bottom you'll find three buttons, labelled File System, Graphics and Virtual Memory. Click the Graphics button and set the slider control to Full hardware acceleration. Don't change this unless you're experiencing screen problems such as a disappearing cursor.

Click the Virtual memory button and ensure that the recommended option, which is to let Windows manage virtual memory, is selected. There is no point specifying your own memory settings unless you're a system administrator troubleshooting a problem.

Clicking the File System button reveals another tabbed dialog box. After making

changes to any of these click the Apply button before moving to the next. If you forget, your changes won't take effect. On the Hard Disk tab change the typical role of the PC from Desktop computer to Network server (this improves file access even if you're not networked) and make sure read-ahead optimisation is set to full.

On the CD-ROM tab set the supplemental cache size to large and set the access pattern for Quad-speed or higher. On the Removable Disk tab you should enable write-behind caching to speed the operation of removable disk drives. Even if you don't have any, ticking this box won't do any harm.

Leave the Troubleshooting tab alone. All the boxes on this tab should be left unticked. Changing any of them is likely to decrease system performance rather than improve it. After making all the required changes close the System Properties box. If you've made changes on the File System button you'll be prompted to restart Windows, which is essential if you want the changes to take effect immediately.

These days you can't buy CD-ROMs as slow as quad speed, and some are as fast as 52-speed. Though not all CD-ROMs are labelled with a speed (or even a make), it's safe to assume it will be quad speed or higher unless your PC is over five years old.

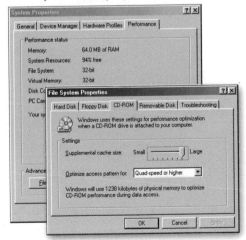

In the System Properties box, beneath the several status lines, is a message which should say that your system is configured for optimal performance. Don't take this at face value. It means there are no major problems with your PC, not that it is tweaked to perfection.

Device Manager settings

Device Manager is one of the tabs in the System Properties box. You may have noticed it while changing Performance settings as described in the preceding section. It tells you more about the components inside your PC or plugged into the back of it. The easiest way of finding the information you need is to click View devices by type, which presents the components in alphabetical order.

Direct memory access

Just as you can enable direct memory access for CD-ROMs (see page 38), you can enable it for hard disks and removable disks. Double click Disk drives in Device manager to see a list of the drives inside your machine. There'll be at least two (one hard and one floppy) and there'll be entries for any secondary hard disks and removable disks you may have. Double click each drive in turn, then click the Settings tab. If

there's a box labelled DMA, tick it. If there's a box labelled Removable and the drive is indeed removable (Zip, LS-120, SuperDisk etc) then tick this too. Don't tick Removable for ordinary fixed hard disks.

Cache settings

If you have lots of spare hard disk space, and this is quite common on new PCs because high-capacity hard disks are amazingly cheap these days, you might decide to use some of it as cache. As in real life, a cache is a store, where you keep things safe until you need them. Two of the most important caches are for Internet Explorer and the Recycle Bin. In the Internet Explorer cache are details of the websites you've visited recently, and if you go back to a site that's already in the cache it doesn't have to be downloaded again. The cache for the Recycle Bin works differently. It's where deleted items are stored until you decide to permanently remove them by emptying the Recycle Bin. If you have a small cache for this purpose you'll be told when you try to delete a very large file that it's too big for the Recycle Bin and can't be recovered if you change your mind.

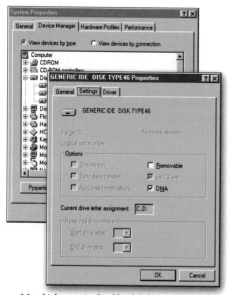

Most high capacity fixed hard disks are type 46 and should have DMA enabled. This one has been split into two logical drives (C: and D:) by a process called partitioning, but physically it's a single unit so the same DMA setting controls both drives.

Find out how big your hard disk is and how much is free. In My Computer, right click drive C: and select Properties. Note that there's a button in this dialog box to start Disk Cleanup if you want to create more space.

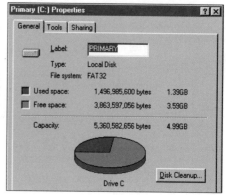

Using spare disk space for Internet Explorer's cache means you'll be able to browse the web faster – and save on phone bills – while a larger Recycle Bin cache means you can work safe in the knowledge that files can be recovered if you delete them by mistake. On the other hand, if you're down to your last 100Mb of disk space you might decide to reduce cache sizes to reclaim disk space.

Adjust Internet Explorer's cache

Start Internet Explorer, open the Tools menu and select Internet Options. Click the General tab and you'll see a panel labelled Temporary Internet Files. Click the Settings button. This reveals a slider control with which you can select how much of drive C: to reserve for the cache. Alternatively, you can specify an exact number of megabytes in the box to the right of the slider.

If you have several gigabytes of spare hard disk space you should allocate around 1Gb (1024Mb) to the cache. If you have less than 1Gb of spare hard disk space try to allocate at least 50Mb to the cache, and more if you frequently download web pages for offline viewing.

Adjusting the Recycle Bin size

Right click the Recycle Bin on the Desktop and select Explore. This displays the contents of the bin in Windows Explorer and you'll be able to see how much space the recycled files are claiming from the status line at the bottom. Right click the Recycle Bin again and select Properties. On the Global tab of the Properties sheet select the option to configure drives independently rather than use one setting for each drive, then click Apply. The advantage of this is that when you click the tab for each drive you'll be able to see how many megabytes are being set aside as you adjust the slider.

A large cache leads to increased security

and peace of mind rather than speed, but if your computer is slowing down because it's running short of disk space you should empty the Recycle Bin and set a smaller cache size to increase the space available for other purposes.

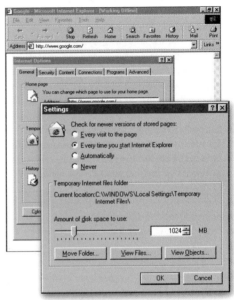

A large Internet Explorer cache speeds up web browsing, and so does making the right choice of when to check for newer versions of stored pages. Selecting Automatically is good for most users, but the fastest setting is Never. The snag is you then have to click the Refresh button on the IE toolbar whenever you want to see an updated version of a web page.

Don't worry if the size of your hard disk is incorrectly reported in Recycle Bin Properties. This is a well-known and harmless Windows bug. If you're desperately short of disk space click the box to disable the Recycle Bin and remove files immediately when deleted.

Changing to 32-bit file access - step by step

32-bit file access is one of the major features of Windows 98. It's a more efficient way of organising files on a hard disk and it not only makes a disk faster but also increases its capacity. The alternative is the 16-bit file system used by Windows 95. When you save a file on a 2Gb Windows 95 disk it occupies at least 32Kb, even if it's a one-word text file from Notepad and its size is reported in Explorer as just a few bytes. By switching to 32-bit file access the minimum space occupied by a file is reduced from 32Kb to 4Kb, which greatly reduces waste and enables more to be stored on a disk.

1 Despite its benefits, 32-bit file access may not have been enabled on your PC, either because Windows 98 was installed as a Windows 95 upgrade or because the maker of your PC chose not to use it.

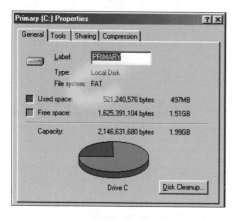

To check your hard disk, double click My Computer on the Desktop then right click drive C: and select Properties. If the file system is reported simply as FAT it means 32-bit file access has not been installed.

2 If the file system is reported as FAT32 there is nothing more to be done. Otherwise you should proceed to convert your drive by starting Drive Converter. You'll find it on the Start button by selecting Accessories and System Tools. Click Drive Converter (FAT32) to start it.

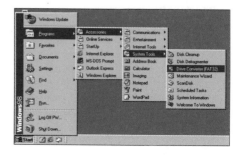

3 In Drive Converter, click the Details button on the opening screen. This provides more information about how 32-bit file access works and describes

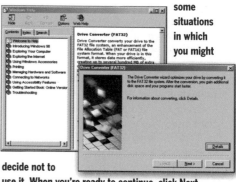

some situations in which you might decide not to use it. When you're ready to continue, click Next.

4 On this screen you select which drive you want to convert. Drives must be converted one at a time so if you have more than one you'll have to run Drive Converter once for each. The drive that will yield the greatest benefit from conversion is the one on which Windows is installed – usually this is drive C.

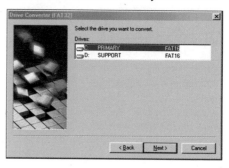

5 Drive Converter checks whether you're running any programs incompatible with 32-bit file access such as obsolete disk utilities and out-of-date anti-virus programs. All current versions of such products work fine on FAT32 drives. You'll also receive a

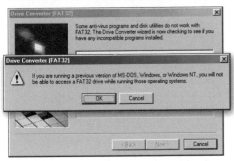

warning that if you are running previous versions of MS-DOS, Windows or Windows NT you won't be able to access the FAT32 drive. Obviously, if you're using Drive Converter you've got Windows 98, so the warning is really for those on a network who might want to use ANOTHER computer to get at the files on this drive.

6 After passing through several information screens you'll be asked if you'd like to back up the drive before converting it. Even though converting to FAT32 is not a risky procedure it's always advisable to back up a hard disk before making major changes to it. Unfortunately, when you click the Create Backup button you may be faced with the message shown here. Drive Converter contains no backup facility of its own and if Windows Backup is not already installed, now is hardly the best time to grap-

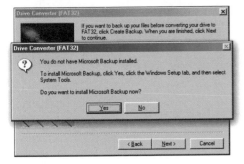

ple with it. Better to back up the hard disk before running Drive Converter, not at this late stage.

7 Drive Converter needs to restart Windows in order to do its job. Checking the integrity of the disk and performing the conversion takes only a few minutes but when Windows restarts Disk Defragmenter immediately kicks in to close up the gaps on the disk, a process that could take several hours. If you

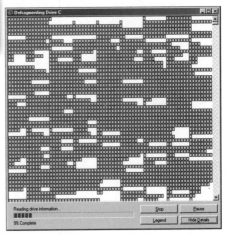

can't spare the time straight away you can cancel Disk Defragmenter and run it later, but don't forget to do this before too long because, as shown above, there are lots of gaps to be closed.

8 Comparing the converted drive below with the FAT16 version in step 1 shows the space-saving benefits of conversion. Though the total capacity of the disk has

barely changed, the 497Mb of used space has been drastically reduced to 395Mb. This is in addition to the speed benefits conferred by Windows now being able to handle information in 4Kb chunks instead of 32Kb.

CHAPTER 7 Troubleshooting

Sounds good, doesn't it? Troubleshooting – the sort of thing Clint Eastwood would be good at. In fact, troubleshooting Windows doesn't require heroic effort because there are plenty of tools hidden within Windows to help revive an ailing PC.

Is Windows reliable?

Given that Windows is an immensely complicated piece of software written by hundreds, probably thousands, of people over a period of years it inevitably contains flaws – or bugs as they're more commonly called. When these come to light Microsoft corrects them by issuing patches or upgrades. There's actually not much difference between the two except that a patch fixes a dodgy program and an upgrade replaces it.

Even in its unpatched state Windows is stable, but it would be unduly optimistic to say that problems are unlikely to arise. The only way to keep Windows in pristine condition is to install it perfectly and then never change anything, but this is not how people use their PCs. They download files from the internet, add new hardware to their machines

and install new programs as a matter of course. When problems do occur, the cause can often be traced to a recently installed program that has replaced a Windows file with a newer or older version of the same file. Just because the new program works perfectly with the replacement Windows file doesn't mean that all the old ones will, but fixing the problem may involve nothing more than reinstalling the original file. The trick, of course, is finding what needs fixing.

Windows is packed with troubleshooters. These are the ones built into Windows Me, but Windows 98 is almost equally well endowed.

If the write protect tab on a floppy disk covers the cut-out you can record new data onto it and delete what's already there. But, slide the tab to reveal the cutout and the contents of the disk are protected against alteration and erasure.

When a problem leads to an error message you're well on the way to solving it, especially if it's not really a problem but an attempt by you, the user, to do something impossible. For example, everybody at some time tries to copy a large file onto a disk that's not big enough to take it it, or attempts a save onto on a floppy disk that's not formatted or has had its write protect tab enabled. Formatting, if you've never heard of it, is the process of preparing a floppy disk for use by laying magnetic tracks on it. These days it's usually done at the factory but at one time you had to do it yourself.

When an error message says, 'The disk in the destination drive is full. Insert a new disk to continue,' it's absolutely clear what the problem is and how to solve it. Less clear is a message like, 'A filename cannot contain any of the following characters: \ /:*?<>_' You get this when you try to save a document with forbidden characters in the file name.

Why are they forbidden? Because Microsoft says so. Just change the name to remove the offending character and save again.

Misleading and unhelpful

Some error messages appear to be helpful but they're not. A message box labelled Out of Memory and containing the message, 'Your computer does not have enough available memory to complete this task,' sounds as if it's a clear instruction to go out and buy some, but in fact it's usually caused by a program failing to find a big enough chunk of memory in the right place. There may be plenty of memory available but the program can't use it. The solution here is not to buy more memory but to close down Windows and restart it. If you know which program caused the message, run it before loading other programs.

The most misleading of all messages is, 'This program has performed an illegal operation and will be shut down. If the problem persists, contact the program vendor.' What this really means is, 'We don't know what happened. Keep your fingers crossed and hope it doesn't happen again. If it does, don't bother us.'

This error message comes not from Windows but from Paint Shop Pro. The invalid parts of the name are the separators in the date, which could be replaced with dashes, as in 2-7-2000.

Identify problems (continued)

The illegal operation is doubly confusing. Not only is the exact nature of the problem not specified, neither are you told who to contact. The name of the offending program is displayed in the error message title bar, but a program's file name is seldom the same as its everyday name. For example, the main program file for Microsoft Word is Winword. You might manage to work this one out for yourself, but what about Psp and Wpwiz? The first is the popular Paint Shop Pro graphics program and the second is the Web Publishing Wizard in Windows.

To track down the file causing an error message use the Find feature on the Start button (Search in Windows Me) and look for the name shown in the error message title bar. This will lead you to the folder containing the file, which should identify the program. Before you contact the program's vendor make sure you can provide information about the hardware in your PC (processor type, amount of memory, graphics card, size of hard disk) which version of Windows you're running, which version of the offending program, and the circumstances in which the error occurs.

Blue screens and lock-ups

A blue screen error message is rare but unmistakable. You don't see a typical Windows message-in-a-box, instead the screen turns completely blue and a terse text message tells you there's a problem. If it's an exception error in a VxD the problem is related to hardware drivers and the troubleshooters described on the next page should be able to confirm this, a parity error could mean faulty memory chips (contact the computer vendor) and other problems may be related to disk and file errors (see page 54).

A lock-up is different. When it happens, a program simply stops responding. Mouse and keyboard commands have no effect but you don't receive any error messages. Lockups may affect a single program or they may affect several at the same time, and the best way to deal with them is with a three-fingered salute. In other words, hold down the Control and Alt keys, then tap Delete. In MS-DOS this causes a PC to reboot but in Windows it's used to display the Close Program dialog box.

If the Close Program dialog box lists a program with 'Not Responding' next to it, highlight the program and click the End Task button. If after a short wait another dialog box appears, click End Task again.

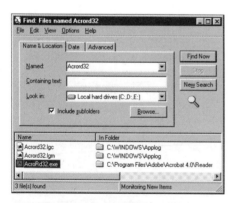

Using the Find facility to track down an error with Acrord32 tells us that the offending program is Adobe Acrobat Reader. Programs can be distinguished from other files with similar names by their three-letter extensions of COM or EXE.

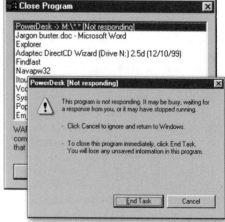

Solving problems

After using End Task to shut down a program in the Close Program dialog box, it's a good idea to save the work in all the other open programs, then close them down all in the usual manner and restart Windows. Many errors are transitory, caused by different programs that are competing for the same area of memory. Closing down and restarting clears the memory and gives every program a fresh chance to grab its own space in memory.

Hardware problems

All versions of Windows have troubleshooters to lead you step-by-step through fixes for common problems with hardware and software. To see which troubleshooters are available in your version of Windows click the Help button on the Start menu, then in Windows 95 and Window 98 click the Index tab and type 'troubleshooting'; in Windows Me use the Search panel to find 'troubleshooters'. If the list of troubleshooters seems daunting because you don't know

As well as looking in Device Manager for exclamations marks and crosses that indicate a component isn't working, also check that a device isn't listed twice or completely omitted.

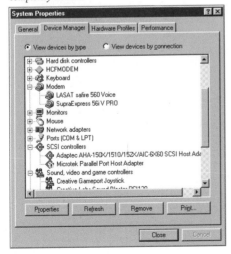

where to start, you might get a clue from Windows Device Manager. Right click My Computer on the Desktop, select Properties, then click the Device Manager tab. If there's a problem with any piece of hardware it has a yellow exclamation mark next to it. If it is working but has been disabled it will have a red cross through it.

Corrupted programs

A corrupt program is one that's been changed in some way since it was installed. It could be that one of the files required by the program has been accidentally renamed, or it may indicate a physical problem with the hard disk. The most unlikely reason for a corrupted program is that it has been attacked by a virus. This is often the first thing most people worry about but if you have an anti-virus program installed and you keep it up to date the chances of attack are remote.

Some corrupted programs won't run at all, others may start to load but then crash. One clue that a program has become corrupted is an error message saying that it's not a valid Win32 application. Clearly it was the last time you ran it, which must mean it has been changed since.

Sometimes a program becomes so corrupted that Windows thinks it's an MS-DOS program and runs it. This usually results in a jumble of hieroglyphics like below. The only way to fix a program this badly damaged is to reinstall it from its original CD-ROM or disks.

Disk and file errors

The most obvious clue that all is not well with Windows is when ScanDisk runs when you switch on your PC. ScanDisk's mission in life is to check whether files have been stored correctly on a hard disk and check the surface of a disk for physical damage. It can repair errors if it finds then.

When ScanDisk runs by itself before Windows starts, it does so because the PC was turned off without choosing Shut Down from the Start menu. This might have been the result of forgetfulness, power failure or an act of desperation because nothing else seemed to be working.

Nine times out of ten you can get away with quitting Windows without closing it down properly, but sometimes ScanDisk finds that files have been left open (changed but not saved) and has to sort them out. When this happens it usually manages to recover the situation and get Windows going but there's no guarantee that every file you were working on will be rescued, and if you're very unlucky Windows might refuse to start. The lesson is that prevention is definitely better than cure and you should never switch off your PC without shutting down, except when there's no alternative.

This is what Scandisk looks like when it runs outside Windows. If it doesn't run automatically you can start it from the MS-DOS prompt by typing Scandisk and pressing Enter. It's far easier to use from within Windows so the MS-DOS version is for emergencies.

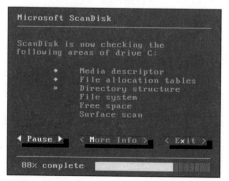

ScanDisk

ScanDisk can do more than rescue the situation as a result of Windows having been closed down abnormally. This utility program can also sort out all kinds of disk and filing problems and should be the first tool that you turn to whenever programs either refuse to load, or lock up without displaying any helpful error messages.

You'll find ScanDisk on the System Tools menu and it can also be started by double clicking My Computer on the Desktop, then right clicking any drive icon and clicking the Properties sub-menu. Select the Tools tab and use the Check Now button. Once ScanDisk has started select the disk you want to check from the drop-down list, select Standard as the type of test required and put a tick in the box that's labelled Automatically fix errors. That's all there is to it. Choosing Thorough rather than Standard checks the disk surface as well the files, but might take many hours.

The advantage of starting ScanDisk from My Computer is that it shares a Properties sheet with Disk Defragmenter and Microsoft Backup, two other disk-related tools.

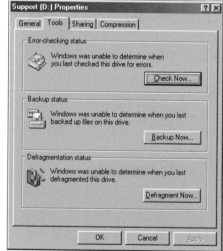

Making a Startup disk

A Windows Startup disk is a floppy disk containing enough programs to start your PC when Windows won't work. It's not the same thing as the Windows Boot Disk, which is the one you use to install Windows for the first time; the Startup disk is made for you by Windows during the installation process. If you don't have one it's crucial to make one as soon as possible.

Making a Startup disk

Open Control Panel and double click Add/Remove programs. We've already used this dialog box to add Windows components, but on this occasion click the Startup disk tab. You'll be asked to insert your Windows CD-ROM and you'll then have to wait a minute of so while files are prepared. You'll then be asked to label and insert a floppy disk. A used disk will do but don't use one that has anything you need on it because the existing contents will be wiped.

Using a Startup disk

A clear signal that it's time to dig out the Startup disk is when Windows won't start at all, or when it tries to but fails. In this case switch off your PC, insert the Startup disk in the floppy drive, then switch on again.

You'll see a lot of activity on screen, and if it's a Windows 98 Startup disk a driver will be loaded for the CD-ROM drive and an

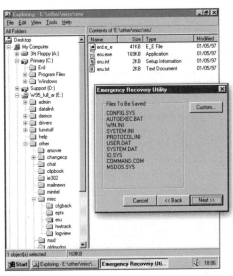

For Windows 95 users only there's a utility on the CD-ROM called the Emergency Recovery Utility (ERU). You'll find it in the folder called \other\misc\eru on the CD-ROM. Double click eru.exe and choose whether you want to create a floppy disk or store the recovery files in a folder on the hard disk.

extra virtual disk drive containing utility programs will be created. This has the effect of moving the CD-ROM drive one letter on, so if it was D: in Windows 98 it will be E: when using the Startup disk. A Windows 95 Startup does not create a virtual disk, nor does it load a driver for the CD-ROM, which is inactive when using a Startup disk.

The first task after starting your PC is to run a comprehensive ScanDisk session by specifying a full unattended check. You can do so by typing the following:

ScanDisk C:/autofix/nosave/nosummary/surface

Then press Enter. This will check and automatically fix any filing errors, then continue with a full disk surface check, which might take hours. To skip the surface check omit '/surface' from the command line.

A Windows Startup disk is NOT an alternative to a backup. It does not store any document files, so if there's work on your PC you simply couldn't bear to lose you need a full backup on disk or tape as well as your Startup disk.

Using a Startup disk

When ScanDisk has finished remove the Startup disk and switch off your PC. Wait a few seconds before switching it on again. If Windows starts the problem has been fixed by ScanDisk. If it still won't start and you've got Windows 98, try again but this time hold down the Control key. If you're a Windows 95 user watch the screen carefully and when you see the message 'Starting Windows 95' hold down function key F8.

After several seconds either of these actions produces the Windows Startup menu. From this you can attempt to start Windows in Safe mode in which all the

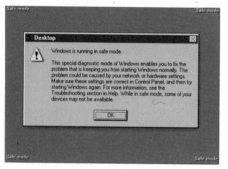

inessential drivers are ignored, thus making Windows less likely to fail. Safe mode is the third option on the Startup menu. Type 3 and press Enter.

If Safe mode starts this is a big step forward. Unless you're a computer wizard there's little you can do to fix Windows when it's in Safe mode, but the very act of starting it clears a number of Windows settings and often makes a normal boot possible thereafter. Once Safe mode has loaded, click OK, then shut down in the usual way and try to start Windows again.

Restoring system files

If Windows still won't start you have a serious problem on your hands. If you've got a backup of the entire hard disk and the backup program runs from MS-DOS

you should use it. If your backup program works only from Windows you won't be able to use it, in which case the only move left to you is to replace the system files on the hard disk (which might have been damaged) with good ones from the floppy disk.

To do this, start the PC with the Startup disk in the floppy drive and when it has finished loading type:

Sys c:

Press Enter. When you see the message 'System transferred', remove the floppy disk and try starting Windows again. If it still won't start then it's time to seek expert help. Alternatively, if you have Norton SystemWorks or a similar utility program you could try its emergency startup disks.

Safe mode is only safe because all the potentially harmful bits have been removed. Oddly, this makes is really hard to solve problems in Safe mode because none of the usual drivers are loaded and many diagnostic programs won't work.

A program like Norton SystemWorks not only provides tools to help you recover a damaged system, it includes protective features like CrashGuard that work within Windows to prevent disastrous situations occurring.

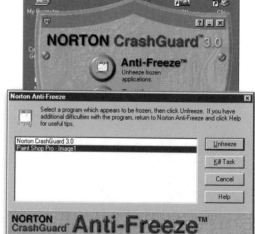

56

Using System File Checker - step by step

Windows 98 lacks the Emergency Recovery Utility of Windows 95 because it incorporates similar features within the main operating system. In the same way, the System File Checker of Windows 98 has been superseded in Windows Me by built-in capabilities. Nevertheless System File Checker is an amazingly useful tool for repairing a damaged version of Windows 98: one that may once have worked perfectly but has become unstable after too many programs have made changes to it. If you're a Windows 98 user here's how to use System File Checker to restore Windows 98 to peak condition.

1 System File Checker is part of the multi-talented System Information utility. You'll find it by clicking the Start button followed by Programs, Accessories and System Tools. Double clicking System Information starts the program and displays a screen telling you when and how Windows was first installed, plus several other useful facts about your PC including whether it is using FAT32 and how

much memory is installed. System Information can tell a trained engineer just about everything there is to know about a PC, but for the ordinary user the real gems are on the Tools menu. One of these is System File Checker.

2 The opening screen of System File Checker offers just two options: Scan for altered files and Extract one from installation disk. Until you know

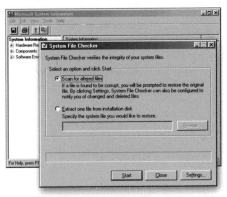

which files may have been altered you can't sensibly use the second option so if this is your first encounter with System File Checker select Scan for altered files and click Start.

3 A search is carried out for Windows files that have changed since the last time you ran Windows Setup, Windows Update or used Add/Remove programs. Files are checked by comparing them with a verification file stored in the Windows folder. When a file is found to have changed or is suspected of being corrupted you have three alternatives.
● If you know the file has been replaced with a newer version select Update verification information.
● If you want to revert to the original version you should select the Restore file option.
● If you want to ignore the fault at this time (possibly until you see how many other files have been changed) select Ignore.
Click OK.

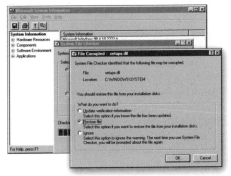

Using System File Checker (continued)

4 Here we've chosen to restore the original version of setupx.dll. Actually this is a file that System File Checker is almost bound to highlight every time you run a check, but it's a good one to practise on! The Restore File dialog asks you to specify where the original file can be found and where it should go. The destination of C:\Windows\System is correct but you may need to change the source if your CD-ROM drive is shown incorrectly.

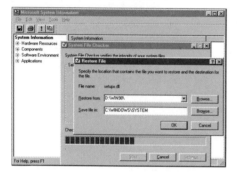

5 Before making a replacement, System File Checker asks if you'd like to keep a backup copy of the existing verification file, just in case you later decide to revert to it. This is a good idea and the suggested location of C:\windows\helpdesk is as good as any. Click OK. When all the files have been checked you can choose to view the details of changes that have been made or simply click OK to finish.

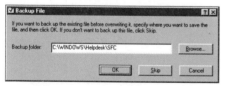

6 If replacing files in this manner doesn't solve whatever problems you've been having, restart System File Checker and on the opening screen click the Settings button. On the Settings tab tick the boxes labelled Check for changed files and Check for deleted files. On the Advanced tab click the Restore defaults button and, if necessary, enter the location of the Windows CD-ROM. Start the check.

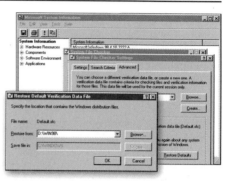

7 The options you've chosen have restored the original verification file from the Windows CD-ROM and the checker is now going to highlight every Windows system file that has been changed, added or deleted.

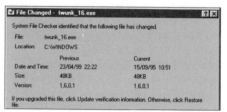

You're going to decide what to do with each. In the example above, a file called twunk_16.exe dated April 1999 has been replaced with an older version dated September 1995. However, as the sizes and version numbers of the files are the same they're clearly identical so you can click Ignore.

8 The original version of ils.dll from April 1999 has been replaced in December 1999 by an older version of the file, which is of a different size and has an earlier version number. In a case like this select Restore file. Substituting all suspect files in this way may be tedious but it's much easier than reinstalling Windows and all your programs from scratch.

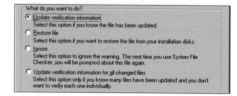

CHAPTER 8 **Tips and tricks**

Tips are ways of doing things with Windows that may be new to you. Tricks are slightly more devious techniques that make Windows do things its designers never intended. A classic tip, and one that can be explained in very few words, is that you can minimise every Window of every open application and get quickly to the Desktop simply by holding down the Windows key and tapping key M. A typical trick, and one that we especially like, is changing the Windows Startup screen to one of your own design. You can find out how to do this on page 65.

The feature that tips and tricks have in common is that they're completely safe and can't harm your PC, so you don't have to worry about losing any work. If they don't work, they don't work. The potentially dangerous stuff is in the next chapter, which tells you how to edit the Windows registry and which we'd advise you to skip if you don't want to take chances.

Selecting more than one file

In Windows Explorer, and in any open folder on the Desktop, you can select several files by dragging a selection box (also called a marquee) around them. Did you also know that you can select files that are not conveniently arranged side-by-side by holding down the Control key while you click? This works whether you're viewing the files as large or small icons or in List and Detail views.

Tips and tricks

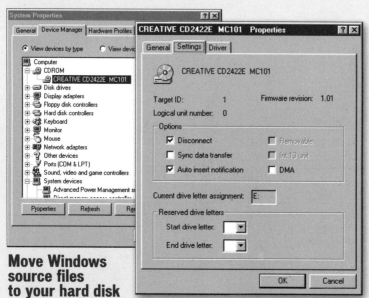

but it's a pain when all you want to do is browse the contents of a disc. To stop a CD-ROM running (or playing if it's an audio CD) hold down one of the Shift keys while closing the CD-ROM tray, and keep it held down for several seconds until the disc activity light stop flashing. If you want to completely disable the autorun facility, right click My Computer and select Properties. Click the Device Manager tab, then double click CD-ROM. When the

Move Windows source files to your hard disk

By copying the Windows source files from their CD-ROM into a folder on your hard disk you will save having to hunt out the CD-ROM every time that you want to add or remove a program or to make a simple change to your system.

The easiest way to copy CD-ROM files is by using Windows Explorer (on the Start button in the Programs group). With the Windows disk in the CD-ROM drive start Windows Explorer and double click the CD-ROM drive. You'll see a folder on the CD-ROM called Win95 or Win98. Drag it to one of the hard disks in your computer, which will have to be Drive C if you have only one.

Remember from now on that the folder called Windows is the installed and working copy of Windows, while the folder called Win95 or Win98 contains the source files that you copied across from the CD-ROM. The other folders on the CD-ROM contain supporting files and drivers that are not needed in normal use. You don't need to copy them.

Disable CD-ROM autorun

When you put a disc in your computer's CD-ROM drive it starts running automatically. This feature makes it easy for beginners to install new programs

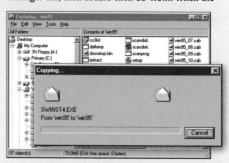

name of your CD-ROM is displayed, double click it to open a Properties dialog box. Then click the Settings tab and remove the tick next to Auto insert notification. Finally, click OK.

Your favourite things

Did you know that if you work on more than one PC you can take your favourites with you? They're stored in a sub-folder of the Windows folder called Favorites, and they'll easily fit onto a floppy disk. Take them with you and copy them into the Favorites folder on the second PC.

Move Desktop icons to the right

By default, icons install themselves on the left-hand side of the Windows Desktop where you can't see them if the Start menu is open. If you'd rather have them on the right-hand side of the Desktop all you have to do is drag a selection box around them and move them over, but first make sure that Auto Arrange is turned off or they'll snap right back. To turn off Auto Arrange, right click anywhere on the Desktop, select Arrange Icons from the menu and remove the tick next to Auto Arrange.

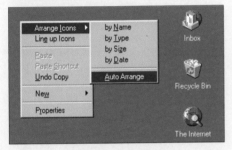

Install CD-ROMs from hard disk

Just as you can copy Windows files to a hard disk, so you can copy the entire contents of any CD-ROM. The advantage of this is that you can then run the CD's Setup program from the hard disk and, with any luck, the installed program will run without the

original CD-ROM being in the drive.

This is particularly useful for encyclopaedias and route finders, where the disc is usually required whenever the program is run. Unfortunately the technique doesn't work with many games because, to prevent software piracy, they're specifically designed not to be used in this way. However, if you've got a massive hard disk with lots of unused space this is a very sensible way of filling it, and even if a program refuses to run it doesn't hurt to try.

In Windows Explorer simply create a folder on your hard disk, then click the CD-ROM drive and select all the files it contains and drag them from the right-hand pane of Explorer into the new folder. Incidentally the shortcut way of selecting every file is to hold down the Control key and press A. The screenshot (below, left) shows Microsoft Office being copied into a hard disk folder called Office.

View Properties for several drives

To see how much space has been used on a drive you can right click its icon in the My Computer window. A neat twist on this technique is to drag a selection box round several drives in My Computer, then select Properties. This produces a box with a separate tab for each drive, and it works for CD-ROM and removable disk drives too!

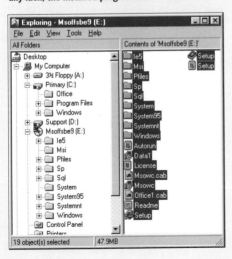

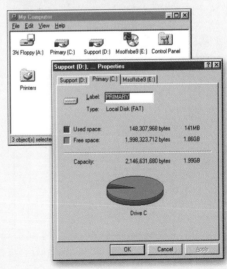

Tips and tricks

Desktop printing and copying

If you put a shortcut to your printer on the Desktop you can print files by dragging them to the printer icon and dropping them. Files can copied by dragging them to disk drive icons. To create a shortcut to your

printer, click the Start button, select Settings, then click Printers. Drag the printer icon onto the Desktop. Windows will tell you the item can't be moved or copied there and will ask you if you'd like a shortcut instead. Click Yes. Drives can be dragged from My Computer to the desktop in a similar manner.

Get hold of TweakUI

TweakUI (the UI part stands for User Interface) is a program that lets you change Windows features you

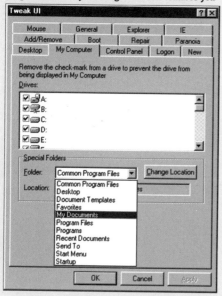

can't get at in ordinary ways. It was designed by Microsoft and originally distributed as one of the Powertoys – programs given away by Microsoft without support or warranty.

Microsoft dropped the Powertoys and TweakUI at about the same time that Windows 98 was released. The good news is that Tweak UI is back, and it's better than ever. It can be downloaded free of charge from: www.microsoft.com/ntworkstation/downloads/Powe rToys/Networking/NTTweakUI.asp. The version number is 1.33 and although it's on the NT website it works with Windows 95, 98 and Windows Me. Once you've downloaded it, double click the file to unzip it, then right click Tweakui.inf and select Install. TweakUI adds itself to Control Panel and you can do things with it like change the location of My Documents, log on without having to type your name, and remove the shortcut arrow from Desktop icons.

Calculated to please

If you've looked at Windows Calculator and then ignored it as being less powerful than the one on your desk or in your pocket, take another look. Start Calculator by opening the Start menu, selecting Accessories and clicking Calculator. To see it in its full glory click the View menu and switch to Scientific mode. To make it easier to use there's a host of shortcut keys (check out the Help screen) and you can find out what all those mysterious buttons do by right clicking and selecting 'What's This?'

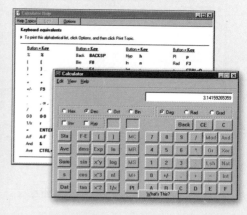

Computer on a toolbar

This one is for Windows 98 users only. It's an even better way of using drag and drop to copy files. Move the My Computer icon to one side of the screen and release it. You'll end up with something just like the Desktop taskbar but containing icons for all My Computer's drives and folders. If you'd rather have text labels than icons drag the My Computer to the top of the screen and not to one side.

The same trick works with Network Neighborhood. Once you've created a My Computer or Network Neighborhood taskbar you can drag it onto the Desktop if you'd rather view it as a panel. To drag a taskbar hold the mouse cursor over its 3D separator bar until it turns into a double-headed arrow.

Send to more than Floppy disks

When you right click on a file and select Send To from the pop-up menu, you're offered a choice of destinations for the file. In Windows 95 the only

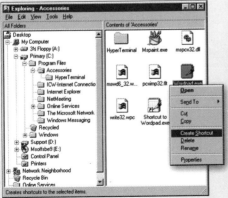

destination you get by default is Floppy (A) but other programs may add their own locations to the list. You can add your own personal choice of programs, disks or folders by creating a shortcut to the item and then placing its shortcut in the Send To folder. Here's how you can add WordPad to the Send To list, which gives you a quick way of opening many types of document file.

Start Windows Explorer and locate the Program Files folder. Double click it to open it, then double click Accessories to reveal WordPad.exe in the right hand pane. Right click Wordpad.exe and select Create Shortcut. When the shortcut has been created drag it to the Send To folder, which is an ordinary sub-folder of Windows.

Taskbar speaker control

If you click the little speaker icon on the taskbar at the bottom of the Desktop you can adjust the volume of your speakers. If you click it and then tick the Mute box you can silence your speakers completely. The icon can be removed if your system has the luxury of a hardware volume control. Simply right click the speaker icon and select Adjust Audio Properties, then remove the tick next to Show volume control on the taskbar.

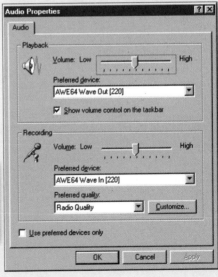

Tips and tricks

Foolproof file rename

Have you ever tried to click on an already selected file to rename it and accidentally loaded it? So have we. A better way to rename a file is to right click and select Rename, or simply press function key F2.

Select Desktop items more quickly by using the keyboard

Did you know you can select Desktop items and shortcuts by clicking on the blank Desktop and pressing the initial letter of the item? In fact, if you've just gone to the Desktop by using the Windows-M shortcut key you don't even have to click the Desktop first. If several shortcut items begin with the same letter just keep pressing the initial key to cycle through them all.

Run two instances of Explorer

Dragging a file within Windows Explorer can be awkward because it's not always possible to make both the source and destination folders visible at the same time. One solution is to start Windows Explorer twice (it's perfectly happy with this) then right click the Desktop taskbar and select Tile Horizontally. You can then drag files from one instance of Explorer to the other.

Changing a file association

Files are associated with programs and Windows knows which program to use for a specific file by examining the file extension. The extension is the second part of file's name and it usually has just three letters (.DOC

for Word, XLS for Excel, BMP for Paint etc).

Sometimes you want to open a file with a different program to the one Windows normally uses. One way of doing this is to start the program first, then load the file. Another way is to select the file, then right click while holding down the Shift key. The effect of holding down Shift is to add an Open With command to the context menu. Click this and you'll be presented with a full list of programs that Windows recognises. Choose the one you want to use, and if you'd like it to become the new default program for that type of file, tick the box next to 'Always use this program to open this type of file'.

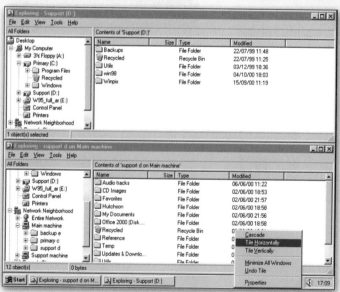

Change the Startup screen - step by step

To create a new Windows opening screen you make a 320-pixel-wide by 400-pixel-tall picture and save it on drive C with the name Logo.sys. The picture must be saved in 256-colour format and be no size other than 320 × 400. You can create such a picture in Windows Paint. If you're feeling very creative you can also change the two closing screens: the one that says 'Windows is shutting down' and the one that says 'It's safe to turn off your computer.' These are stored in Logow.sys and Logos.sys respectively, in the Windows folder.

1 The easiest way to be sure of creating the right sort of picture file is to load Logow.sys from the Windows folder and use it as a template. Run Windows Paint from the Start menu by selecting

Programs, then select Accessories and click Paint. Click the File menu in Paint and select Open. In File name box type C:\Windows\Logow.sys. Click Open.

2 Immediately change the name of the file so that if you make a mess of it you don't overwrite the existing Logow.sys. To do this click Save As on the File menu. In the File name box type C:\ Mylogo.bmp and click Save. Next click Select All on the Edit menu, and with the entire picture thus selected press the Delete key to clear it. You now have a blank canvas on which to create your own opening screen.

3 You will have noticed that the original picture looked very narrow. This is because Windows stretches the opening screen when it displays it, so while you are designing your own screen you must bear this in mind. If it looks good in Paint it will look distorted when Windows uses it. So, think thin! When you've finished being creative click Save on the File menu, then close Paint.

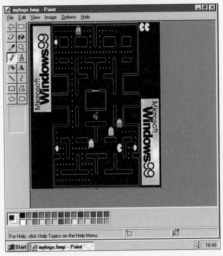

4 To use the screen you've just created it has to replace the existing logo.sys file in the root folder of drive C. If you can't see logo.sys make sure you've enabled the viewing of file extensions and system files as described on page 11. If you still can't see it. don't worry, not all releases of Windows had this file. All that remains is to rename mylogo.bmp as logo.sys, then restart Windows to see the effect.

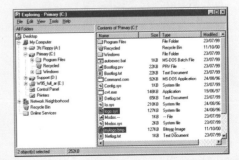

CHAPTER 9

The Windows registry

Don't let the word 'advanced' put you off. You don't need to be a computer wizard to use a number of well-known techniques that give you more control over how Windows works for you. We've kept them together in this chapter to highlight the fact that they should be used carefully, not that they're hard to understand. All of them involve making changes to the Windows registry, which in extreme circumstances could result in Windows not starting properly, but if you follow our advice regarding making copies of the registry you will not find yourself in a position where you can't put things quickly to rights.

The Windows registry

The Windows registry is a complete log of all the separate programs that together make up the Windows operating system. It also contains the settings used by the components inside your PC, details of the programs you've installed and all your preferences and options. It's such an important file that every time you start Windows a copy of the registry is made. Windows 98 stores the five most recent versions of these

and Windows 95 keeps the current version and the previous one. If the registry is damaged through a power cut or disk failure Windows switches to the most recent undamaged one.

If you're going to make alterations to the registry yourself we suggest you make your own copy of it. This is not in case of damage, it's so you can revert to the old version if you change a setting and then wish you hadn't.

In Windows 98 the five most recent copies of the registry are kept in the Window\Sysbckup folder. In Windows 95 the backups (User.dao and System.dao) are in the Windows folder itself.

Safety first with the registry

Copying the registry

Windows comes with a program called Registry Editor for viewing and changing the registry. To use it, open the Start menu and select Run. Type Regedit and click OK. Your first task should be to save a copy of the existing settings by clicking Export Registry File (on the Registry menu) and giving it an unambiguous name such as 'My registry'.

Restoring the registry

In Windows all you need do to restore a registry file and thus reinstate the original settings is start Registry Editor and use

When you export the registry in Windows 95 it is saved by default on the Desktop. This is an excellent place for it because all it takes is a double click to automatically restore the settings it contains.

If a Windows 95 registry becomes so damaged that Windows can't start, restore it from MS-DOS using this sequence of commands. Windows 98 is able to repair a damaged registry without user intervention.

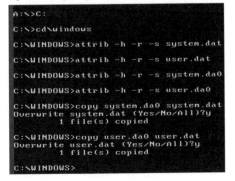

Import Registry File on the Registry menu to load 'My registry' or whatever your copy is called. If Windows won't start because the registry is damaged you can fix this too. Start your PC in MS-DOS mode using a Windows Startup disk (see page 55). Then, if you're a Windows 98 user type the following line and press Enter.

C:\windows\command\scanreg/restore

It's slightly more complicated if you're using Windows 95 but just as foolproof. Type each of the following lines, pressing Enter after each one.

```
c:
cd \windows
attrib -h -r -s system.dat
attrib -h -r -s user.dat
attrib -h -r -s system.da0
attrib -h -r -s user.da0
copy system.da0 system.dat
copy user.da0 user.dat
```

In either case, when you've made the changes switch your computer off and restart it before using Windows.

Changing the registry

You don't need to understand anything about the registry apart from how to make changes to it; then when you come across a registry-based tip in a book, in Computer*Active* magazine or on the web you'll be able to use it. At the end of this chapter on pages 70 and 71 we step you through the entire process of safely carrying out a registry change that adds Open with Notepad to the menu that pops up when you right click on a file. It's just one example of how editing the registry enables you to make changes that are simply not possible by any other means. However, you shouldn't get too carried away with customising your copy of Windows. Other people may want to use it too.

Registry tips and tweaks

The registered Windows owner

If you've bought a second-hand computer on which Windows is registered to somebody else you can change the name of the registered owner. The same applies if you've bought a new PC that's registered to Swizzo Computers, Preferred User or some other anonymous organisation.

Start Registry Editor, then use the plus sign (or double click) to open each of the following entries: **HKEY_LOCAL_MACHINE, Software, Microsoft, Windows**. Click the key in the left hand pane called Current Version and amongst the values displayed on the right you'll see Registered Owner and Registered Organization. Double click these to change them. Exit the editor from the Registry menu.

Personalised opening message

It's possible to display a personalised message box whenever Windows starts and whenever a new user logs on. You can decide what the text in the title bar will be and what the message should say. The box is meant to provide legal warnings but you can use it to greet users with a cheery mes-

sage or ask them to respect the machine by leaving it as they found it.

Start Registry Editor, then use the plus sign (or double click) to open each of the following entries: **HKEY_LOCAL_MACHINE, Software, Microsoft, Windows, Current Version**. Right click the key in the left hand pane called Winlogon and create a new String Value. Call it LegalNoticeCaption (all one word). Right click Winlogon again and create a new String Value called LegalNoticeText (all one word). Double click these entries to enter values. The first determines the title and the second the message.

Create your own Windows tips

Maybe you don't need the Windows tips any more but you'd like to create new ones for other people to read. The tips are registry values you can change by double clicking them. Go to them by starting Registry Editor, then use the plus sign (or double click) to open each of the following entries: **HKEY_LOCAL_MACHINE, Software, Microsoft, Windows, CurrentVersion, Explorer**. Click the key called Tips in the left hand panel to see the text for the tips in the right hand panel.

When creating a personalised opening message try to keep the message within the bounds of what can reasonably be displayed on a single line.

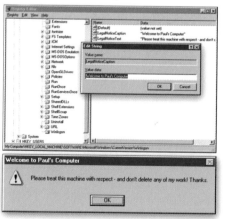

As with all text values entered in Registry Editor, don't type the speech marks yourself. Double click an entry to modify it and then type directly into the Edit String dialog box. Windows will add the speech marks to suit its own purposes.

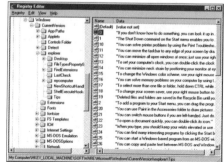

68

Registry tips and tweaks (continued)

Relocate the installation files

There's nothing more annoying than Windows asking for the CD-ROM every time you make a minor change. One solution is to copy the Windows install files from the CD-ROM onto your hard disk, as

By relocating the Windows installation files to the hard disk and modifying this value in Registry Editor Windows will never bother you again for its CD-ROM or help with finding its system files.

suggested on page 60. The snag is that Windows still looks for a CD and you have to redirect it to the hard disk every time, but with a simple registry edit you can tell Windows where to look.

Start Registry Editor, then use the plus sign (or double click) to open each of the following entries: **HKEY_LOCAL_MACHINE, Software, Microsoft, Windows, CurrentVersion**. Click the key in the left hand pane called Setup and then double click the value on the right called SourcePath to change it to wherever you've copied the Windows files.

Clear unwanted entries from Add/Remove programs

If you remove a program by deleting its files instead of uninstalling it properly, its name still appears in Add/Remove programs even though the program itself has gone. You don't have to reinstall it and then uninstall it just to remove its name from the list. Use the following registry edit.

Start Registry Editor, then use the plus sign (or double click) to open each of the following entries: **HKEY_LOCAL_MACHINE, Software, Microsoft, Windows, Current Version, Uninstall**. The name of each program appears as a key in the left hand panel. Right click a program's key and then click Delete on the context menu to remove it.

Stop programs auto-running

As you're probably aware, you can run programs automatically when Windows starts by placing them in the Startup folder. Commercial programs sometimes auto-run

Programs that auto-run themselves from the registry are usually system utilities such as anti-virus tools. However, if a program keeps nagging you to register or mysteriously logs you unwillingly onto the web for updates, look for it here.

themselves when you don't want them to, and unless you know how to delete them they can be a real pain. Here's how to get rid of an automatically running program that's NOT in the Startup folder.

Start Registry Editor, then use the plus sign (or double click) to open each of the following entries: **HKEY_LOCAL_MACHINE, Software, Microsoft, Windows, Current Version**. Click the key called Run in the left hand panel to see a list of the programs that run automatically in the right hand panel. To remove a program, right click on its entry in the right hand panel and select Delete from the context menu.

Changing the registry - step by step

To the ordinary user the context menus that appear in response to a right-button mouse click are fixed in stone. Programs can be neither added nor removed; yet it's obvious that the context menus can be changed because many third-party programs add themselves to the right-button menu when you install them. Here's how to add Notepad to the menu that pops up when you right click on a file.

1 Start Registry Editor by clicking the Start button, then Run. In the box type Regedit and click OK.

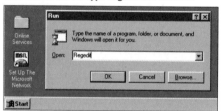

2 Once Registry Editor has started you should immediately make a copy of it. Do this by opening the Registry menu and clicking Export Registry File. Name the file something that clearly tells you when you saved it, such as 'Before adding Notepad to right button', then click the Save button.

3 In the left hand panel of Registry Editor you'll see six categories of settings, beginning with HKEY-CLASSES_ROOT. Next to each category is a plus sign that opens it up. Click the plus sign next to

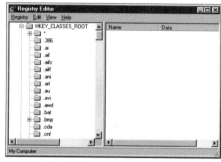

HKEY-CLASSES_ROOT. Immediately beneath this is the first of a long list of folder icons. It has no name but is marked with an asterisk (star).

4 Right click the asterisk folder and select New on the context menu, then click Key. A blank entry for a new key will be created in the left-hand panel of Registry

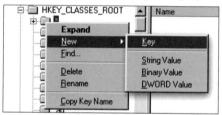

Editor. By default it has the name New Key #1. Type Shell and press Enter. You have just created a new key and named it Shell. Everything in the left hand panel is called a key, while the right hand pane contains values. The Shell key you've just created currently has no value.

5 Right click the Shell key you've just created and make another new key. Change its name from New Key #1 to Open. Then right click the Open key you've just made and create yet another. Call this one Command.

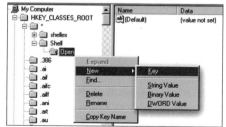

Changing the registry (continued)

6 You've now created three new keys – Shell, Open and Command – but none of them yet has a value. A value can consist of numbers, words or a combination of the two. To create or edit a value you select the key you want to change on the left hand side, then double click its entry on the right hand side. So to give a value to the Open key, you click Open in the left hand pane, then double click Default in the right hand pane. The Edit String box opens. Type 'Open with Notepad' (no quotes required) then click OK.

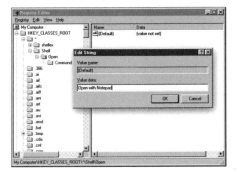

7 All that remains is to give a value to the Command key. Click Command on the left, then double click Default on the right. The value to type (no quotes) is 'C:\Windows\Notepad.exe %1'. Click OK. Well done! You've just changed the registry by adding a command called Open with Notepad to the right button menu.

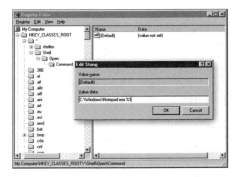

8 If you're at all unsure about what you've just done, simply delete the keys you've added by right clicking them and selecting Delete. Then restore the

original registry by opening the Registry menu and clicking Import Registry File. Select the registry copy you made in step 2 and click Open.

9 Click Exit on the Registry menu, then test the feature you've added to the right mouse button by opening a folder on the Windows Desktop or starting Windows Explorer. Select any file and right click

to check that Open with Notepad has been added to the context menu. Remember that Notepad is a text editor and can't be used to open every type of file, but you'll now be able to open text files with odd names such as Read.me, and many other kinds of log file such as those generated by ScanDisk.

What you've learnt

The techniques you've just practised will enable you to tackle any type of registry tweak. (Many are simple, involving nothing more than finding a key and changing its current value.) You've also learnt how to add new keys, delete unwanted keys and copy the registry.

CHAPTER 10

Reinstalling and backup

Reinstalling Windows may not be something you've ever thought about, especially if your PC came from the factory with Windows already on it and all the other programs preinstalled. It's actually not a difficult process but it takes the best part of a day if you include the time it takes to reinstall all your other programs, re-establish an internet connection and set your preferences.

Reasons to reinstall Windows

Chapter 6 describes many of the symptoms of an ailing Windows system: programs that won't run, lost data, frequent error messages and unexplained lock-ups. Another indication of a tired system is the sneaking feeling that your computer is not as fast as it used to be. This happens to all PCs as their disks fill up and Windows acquires a tangle of extra files. PCs have hardly any mechanical components that suffer from wear and tear, so if the tuning and troubleshooting techniques described earlier in this book don't get your PC running as well as it used to, reinstalling Windows is the next step.

Another reason to reinstall Windows is if you've bought an upgrade. These are available

to take a PC from Windows 95 to 98, from Windows 95/98 to Windows 98 SE (Second Edition), and from any version of Windows to Windows Me (Millennium Edition).

Though there are clear benefits in upgrading from Windows 95 to Windows 98 SE – 32-bit file access, support for USB accessories, increased reliability – the upgrade from Windows 98 to Windows Me has drawbacks as well as advantages, which are discussed in the final chapter of this book.

Running Windows Setup from within an existing version of Windows is pretty much a hands-off affair. Just sit back and enjoy the screen show.

Windows is sold in several versions. The three most common are as a full product, an upgrade or in OEM form. The full version comes boxed with manuals and instructions. An upgrade is similarly boxed but can't be installed unless you have an earlier version of Windows. The OEM (Original Equipment Manufacturers) version is just a CD-ROM and a short booklet. This is the version supplied with most new PCs and does not include support from Microsoft. This is the responsibility of the supplier.

Whichever version you have there are two ways of installing it: either as a clean install (from scratch) or as an upgrade (on top of your existing version of Windows). To clarify this, even if you've bought the upgrade version of Windows you can still do a clean install. It's true that you need to prove your possession of an existing version of Windows but you can do this by inserting your old Windows CD-ROM or floppy disks during the set-up process. It's not a requirement to have the old version installed on your hard disk.

Clean install or upgrade?

Whether it's better to do a clean install or upgrade an existing version of Windows depends on how much work you're prepared to do, how well prepared you are and how

Windows is not one product but many. Any of them may be installed or reinstalled without removing the current version of Windows from the hard disk, thus preserving all existing documents and programs.

much of a mess your PC is in right now.

If you install over an existing version of Windows you'll retain all your programs, preferences and settings, and you can be back in action with a new or refreshed version of Windows within a couple of hours. If you do a clean install you'll also have to reinstall all your other programs and re-establish all your shortcuts, preferences and customisations. Think about this, about all the words you've added to the dictionary in your word processor, all the menus and tool-bars you've customised, all the drivers you've updated over the years and the colour and sound schemes you've painstakingly devised. Are you prepared to go through all this again? If you are you'll almost certainly end up with a more reliable system.

If you've heavily modified your current version of Windows and spent ages setting up programs, can you remember how you did it? If you can't, you should try an upgrade rather a clean install.

Installing over the current version of Windows

If your existing Windows system is very flaky, the chances are that installing over it will do it some good, but there's no guarantee that all its idiosyncrasies will be sorted out. One approach would be to try installing over the top of an existing version first and, if this doesn't produce the desired improvements, bite the bullet and perform a clean install.

Preparing to install

● To fully install Windows 98 requires 400Mb (650Mb for Windows Me), and although less space is required to upgrade an existing system it's not advisable to have less than 200Mb for Windows 98 and 300Mb for Windows Me.

● Read the file called Readme.txt on the Windows CD-ROM. This will point you towards other files containing installation tips and instructions. Readme.txt can be opened with Notepad or by simply by double clicking.

● Run a full virus check and then disable your anti-virus program if you have one. You don't have to remove it altogether, just make sure it's not turned on and that it won't run automatically when Windows reboots.

● If you have any other system-level utili-

ties such as crash protection, uninstallers or system monitors disable these too.

● Make a backup of the existing system in case your computer breaks down part way through the upgrade. Power cuts are not necessarily a disaster because in most cases Windows Setup can pick up after an interruption.

Installing

This is the easy part. On the Start menu click Run, then type D:\Setup (assuming D: is your CD-ROM drive) and press Enter. You'll need to stick around for a few minutes to answer some questions, one of which is whether you want to save the existing system files (Yes if you have lots of disk space, No if you don't). You'll also need a floppy so Windows can make you a Startup disk. When Windows starts copying files you can go and put your feet up for an hour and when you get back Windows will have finished installing itself, rebooted itself several times and should now be displaying the Windows Desktop ready for action.

A fuss-free way of upgrading Windows 98 is to copy the source files from the CD-ROM onto your hard disk. Simply drag the entire Win98 folder onto the Desktop, then open it and double click Setup.exe. The files occupy 180Mb.

Even if you don't have a floppy disk to hand when Windows wants you to make a Startup disk, you must click Next. When you're told to put a disk in the drive you can click Cancel. Don't forget to make a Startup disk later, as described on page 55.

Clean installation of Windows 98

Preparation

The preparations for clean installations of Windows 95 and 98 are similar. (Windows Me is rather different and is discussed in Chapter 11.) Two floppy disks are required. One is the Windows Boot disk supplied with Windows CD-ROMs; the other is a Startup disk you can make yourself as described on page 55. You'll also need your Windows serial number (on the CD case, Microsoft authenticity certificate or the Getting Started guide).

You may need to know the makes and models of the equipment inside your PC if Windows can't work things out for itself – especially the modem, sound and graphics cards. It's also worth recording the makes and models of any accessories plugged into the back of the computer such as monitors, printers and scanners. With any luck Windows will have its own drivers for your equipment but have the originals to hand, just in case.

A clean install involves formatting (blanking) the hard disk, so you'll lose all the documents stored on it as well as the programs. Copy anything you may need in the future onto floppy or removable disks first.

If you've misplaced the manuals for your PC and want to know what's inside it, right click My Computer on the Desktop and check out the components listed there. Make a note of them or use the Print button.

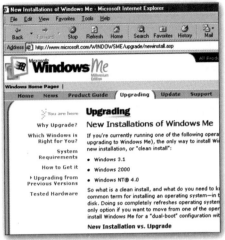

You can upgrade to Windows Me from Windows 95 and Windows 98, but a clean install is required to switch from Windows 3.1, Windows NT or Windows 2000. There's more information on Microsoft's website.

Procedures

When you're ready, put the Startup disk in the floppy drive and switch on your PC. At the opening menu choose option 1 to start the computer with CD-ROM support, then press Enter. At the A: prompt type format C: and press Enter again. You'll be warned that all data will be lost on this drive and you must type Y and press Enter to confirm your acceptance. Formatting takes some time, often many minutes, and at the end you'll be asked to type in a name for the disk. If you don't want to, just press Enter. The hard disk is now blank.

Remove the Startup floppy, switch off the PC and restart it with the Windows Boot Floppy. At the opening menu select option 1 and press Enter. Follow the instructions on screen and when ScanDisk has finished checking your hard disk press X. Windows Setup will then begin. When asked to choose Setup options, select a typical install with the most common components. You can always add to it later.

Back up your troubles

The importance of backing up your hard disk before reinstalling Windows can't be over-emphasised. Throughout this book we've been pointing out the wisdom of making backups, so it's about time we covered the subject in detail.

Backups and copies

There's a difference between a backup and a copy. If you have an important document that must be kept intact you can make a copy of it and store it on a floppy disk (or some either kind of removable disk) and keep it in a safe place. If you lose the original, you can simply retrieve the copy from the spare disk and carry on as if nothing had ever happened.

This principle can be extended to cover all your documents and data. When Windows is installed a folder called My Documents is created. If you keep all the work you produce in this folder it's easy enough to copy its entire contents onto one

A quick way of copying one or more files to a floppy disk is to select a file (or files) on the Desktop, in a window or within Windows Explorer, then right click. On the context menu move the highlight to Send to, where one of options is Floppy (A:). Click to copy the files.

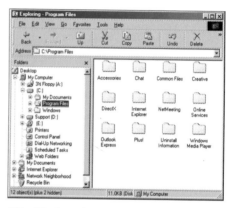

When Windows is first installed, the hard disk (C:) is divided into three primary folders called My Documents, Program Files and Windows. As demonstrated here, there can be many subordinate folders within each of these, but you should try to stick to the original plan.

or more removable disks. Just drag the file, group of files or a folder from one disk to another in Windows Explorer. If there's ever a problem, copy the files back from the removable disks to their original locations.

You can't use the same simple procedures to copy program files or the system files used by Windows itself. It may seem that you can, because there's nothing to stop you copying program files and Windows files onto removable disks, but when you put them back on your hard disk they won't necessarily work.

The reason is that when you install Windows and other programs from their CD-ROMs onto a hard disk they're not simply copied; some of their files are placed in specific locations and recorded in a special way. If you spoil the arrangement they won't necessarily work, which is where backups come in. A backup doesn't just copy files, it copies the way in which the files are arranged on the disk. When you restore a backup, this copies the files and restores their precise relationship with the hard disk and the other files, so they work just as before.

Backing up - step by step

Before you can make a backup you need somewhere to keep it. Floppy disks are out of the question because they don't hold enough data. Removable Zip disks of 100Mb or 250Mb are a possibility but you might need ten or more of them to fully back up a hard disk. Recordable CDs (CD-R or CD-RW) are a cheap form of storage but these hold little more than 500Mb each when used for backing up, and the backup program supplied with Windows doesn't let you swap them part way through, which means you have to make several separate 500Mb back-ups to capture an entire hard disk.

The fastest and easiest backup is one made into a designated backup folder on the hard disk itself, but this is also the least safe because if the disk breaks down or the computer is stolen you lose the backup as well as the original! The safest form of backup is one made onto a special backup drive which uses removable tape cassettes. The snag with these is that, unlike Zip disks and recordable CDs, they can't be used for any other purpose.

1 For the purpose of these steps we created a folder called Failsafe on drive (C:). If you don't have any other form of backup device you can do the same.

Double click My Computer, then double click Drive (C:), select New on the File menu and click Folder. Call the folder Failsafe or any name you prefer.

2 Backup is not part of a typical installation. If it has been installed on your PC you'll find it on the System Tools menu (Start button, Programs, Accessories, System Tools), and if it's not there you

can install it following the instructions on page 7. When you start Backup for the first time you'll see the above message unless you have a special backup tape drive. Click No.

3 On Backup's opening screen you have three choices. Select the first one – Create a new backup job – and click OK. You then have to decide whether to do a full backup of My Computer or whether to back up selected files and folders. When backing up a disk into one of its own folders, as we are, only the second option makes sense. Click Next.

Backing up (continued)

4 The backup Wizard now takes over and presents you with a list of the drives in your PC. Tick drive (C:) to select it and all the folders it contains, then click the plus sign to the left of it to reveal its

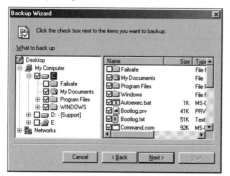

folders. Remove the tick from Failsafe (backing this up onto itself is like a snake trying to swallow its own tail) and click Next.

5 When you're asked whether you'd like to back up all the selected files or just those that have changed, choose all, then click Next. In the future you can keep the backup current by checking for new and changed files on a weekly basis. You now have to choose where to store the backup. The Wizard suggests a file called C:\MyBackup.qic, but we're going to use the Failsafe folder. Click the folder icon next to MyBackup.qic and, when the Wizard displays a list of folders, double click Failsafe then click Open.

6 Click Next and you'll be asked how you want to back up. Two options are available, both of which should be ticked. The first compares the backup with the source files to make sure they've been copied correctly, and the second compresses the files so that the backup requires less space than the original files. Clever stuff! Both these options slow down the backup process but are well worth keeping ticked.

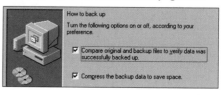

7 All that remains is to type a descriptive name for the backup ('My first backup' will do unless you can think of something better) and click the Start button. You'll have to wait some time for the backup to be made, at least several minutes and perhaps an hour or more, depending on the state of the hard disk and the speed of your PC. Because of the choices you made in step 6 the backup will be verified automatically.

8 On completion, if the Status line says 'Backup completed – Errors reported' click the Report button to see what they are. They're usually caused by programs left running during the backup (Task Scheduler and anti-virus programs are prime offenders). Write down their names and remember next time to close them before running Backup.

Restoring damaged files - step by step

1 To restore files backed up on the previous two pages start Backup, as described on page 77, and on the opening screen select the option to restore backed up files. Click OK. The file most recently saved is high-

lighted, which in this case is the Mybackup.qic file in the Failsafe folder, but you can type another file name or use the folder icon to browse for a different file.

2 When you click Next you're presented with a dialog box in which you choose a backup set. This only makes sense if you've got a backup tape drive with several backups stored on a single tape. If you backed up in accordance with the instructions on the previous two pages you'll have a single backup set called 'My first backup'. Click OK.

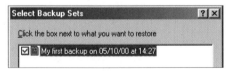

3 When the Restore Wizard starts, no files are selected. In this example we'll pretend the Windows HyperTerminal program has been damaged and we want to restore the original. To do this click the plus

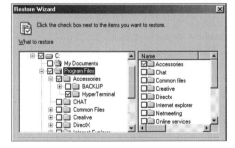

sign next to drive (C:), then the plus sign next to Program Files, and the plus sign next to Accessories. Tick the HyperTerminal box and click Next.

4 The next screen in the Wizard asks where to store the file and suggests the original location, which is what we'll use. If you'd like to store it else-where you can select Alternate location from the drop-down box, then browse for a location by click-ing the folder icon. An different location is usually only necessary when Windows or another program is already using the file you want to restore. Click Next.

5 One decision remains: to instruct the Wizard how to act if a file that's being restored already exists on the computer. The recommended option is not to replace any files that already exist, but as we're pretending the HyperTerminal files are damaged select 'Always replace the file on my computer.' Click Start, and when you're told to insert the required media click OK. A Restore Progress summary will be displayed and the status line should report no errors.

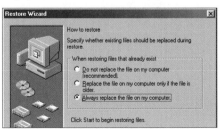

CHAPTER 11

Millennium Edition

Windows Me (Millennium Edition) is the latest addition to the Windows family of operating systems and comes hot on the heels of Windows 2000. Don't confuse the two: Windows Me is sold as a replacement for Windows 98 and is therefore aimed at what Microsoft sees as less demanding users in homes and offices, while Windows 2000 is a replacement for Windows NT and is designed for corporate users, or at least by organisations big enough to have dedicated computer support staff.

In the past new versions of Windows have gradually replaced the older ones, the previous versions remaining on sale until stocks were sold, and this is likely to be the pattern with Windows Me.

Can I buy it now?

Windows Me was launched in September 2000 and is now in the shops. Some PC manufacturers have been installing it on new machines since the day of its release; others are taking a more cautious approach and waiting for updated drivers to become available, while offering Windows Me as an option to those buyers who ask for it.

This book was written entirely using Microsoft Word on a clean installation of Windows Me. We also tested Windows Me as an upgrade to Windows 98 and Windows 95 so we've had plenty of time to sample its new features. As to the question of whether you should upgrade to Windows Me, it's not an easy decision. Why not read the facts and make up your own mind.

The Windows Me Desktop seems completely familiar to users of Windows 95 and 98, but there are new features under the skin and new accessories, such as Windows Movie Maker.

Windows Me doesn't look very different from Windows 95 or Windows 98. A new shade of blue is used for the Desktop; the Recycle Bin and other icons have been tastefully redesigned; and in the Quick Launch area of the taskbar is an additional program, Windows Media Player.

Click the Start button and you'll find that Windows Me has been fitted with the personalised menus of Office 2000, in which seldom-used options are hidden from view but can be made visible by clicking chevrons at the bottom of a menu. Most people turn off this feature in Office 2000 but it works well in Windows Me.

Network Neighborhood has been rebranded as My Network Places and now contains a Wizard to help you set up a home network. My Computer and My Documents are still there, though somewhat changed. Inside My Documents and you'll find three new folders called My Pictures, My Videos and My Music. These serve to emphasise the importance assigned to digital media in Windows Me, as does the inclusion of Media Player as a Quick Launch item.

Menus that adapt themselves to the way you work are a good thing, apart from when you try to rearrange the order of the programs and they seem to disappear!

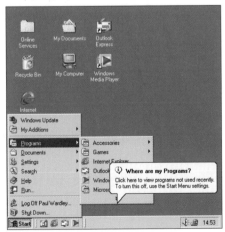

Windows Media Player 7

Launch Media Player and you'll get a surprise. It's a world away from previous versions in terms of its appearance and capabilities, but it's not strictly part of Windows Me because it can be downloaded right now from Microsoft's website for previous versions of Windows.

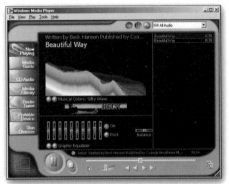

As well as its superior audio features Windows Media Player 7.0 can generate 'visualisations' (pretty moving patterns) that respond to the music.

Windows Media Player 7 can be used to play MPEG video clips and Window video clips in either the old AVI or new WMV formats, music CDs, compressed WMA and MP3 audio files and internet radio stations. You get a graphics equaliser and simulated surround sound effects from twin speaker systems, and the outward appearance of the Media Player can changed by applying 'skins' to the standard player. Many skins are provided and others will be available for download from the web.

DVD movies

Oddly, given the emphasis on digital media and entertainment, Windows Media Player can't play DVD movies. There is a program called DVDplay.exe in the Windows folder, but it doesn't appear on a menu unless you've already got a hardware or software DVD player installed.

Under the surface

If you make a clean install of Windows Me onto a PC with a DVD drive but with no playback hardware you won't be able to play DVD movies – at least not until you've installed a third party software DVD player. Irritatingly, only then will the DVD player in Windows Me kick into action. The thing is, that once you have a commercial player installed it's really not worth using the one in Me. It offers few facilities other than straightforward playback. You can't access special features such as director's comments, cutting from chapter to chapter or alternative screen formats.

You'll never see the DVD movie player built into Windows Me unless you've already got a commercial player of your own, which is about as useful as an extra leg to a centipede.

Disappearing DOS

MS-DOS underlies Windows Me as it does Windows 95 and Windows 98, but Microsoft would like you to think that it doesn't. In Windows Me there is no Exit to MS-DOS option when you leave Windows. Neither can you press Control or F8 while Windows is loading to start at a DOS prompt, and the option of formatting a floppy disk as a system disk has been removed from Disk Format. To get to DOS you have to make an emergency boot floppy disk and start your PC with this in the drive.

The implications of not having easy access to DOS are that it's more awkward to

run backup and restore programs that work outside Windows (as many of them do), and that some programs simply won't work with Me, including anti-virus and system-recovery utilities designed to preload sections of themselves before Windows, and any older DOS games that require you to make a boot disk.

For the first-time buyer with no preconceptions about the relationship between DOS and Windows – and no older programs they'd like to keep using – the sidelining of DOS is probably a good thing, but for the potential upgrader it's something that needs to be considered.

System Restore

A commendable new feature is System Restore. Whenever you make changes to Windows by installing new software or changing optional components Windows creates a restore point. You may also create a restore point yourself at any time you think one is necessary. Then, using System Restore, you can go back to any recent restore point if Windows develops a fault.

System Restore is one of the best things in Windows Me. It doesn't absolve you of the need to make proper backups but it's perfect as a means of rolling back your PC to a time before you unwisely let a computer magazine's cover-mounted CD trash it.

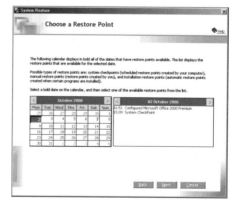

Restoring a system won't recover a document you've lost or damaged. Neither can you go back to a very old restore point because there simply isn't space on a hard disk to store more than a few weeks of roll-back information. Another drawback is that after reverting to a previous restore point you have to reinstall any programs that were added after that date, but despite these limitations System Restore is a useful addition to the armoury of Windows tools. It provides similar features to programs like Go Back and Second Chance, which were clearly the inspiration for System Restore, but these are commercial products that have to be paid for.

System File Protection

This is a feature that has already proved itself in Windows 2000. Microsoft tried something similar in Windows 98 but didn't quite get it right. This time with System File Protection (SFP) the problem of newly installed programs replacing Windows files with earlier or incorrect versions seems to have been cracked. If a program succeeds in overwriting a Windows system file during installation, SFP

System File Protection is something you don't have to worry about. Just be glad it's there, working in the background. However, if you want to know which files aren't protected (because they were already on your PC when you installed Windows Me and are not digitally signed) you can list them.

simply reinstates the correct version. Program makers who want to replace Microsoft system files with different ones have to get the files electronically signed, or tagged, by Microsoft. This protection works even if you try to install older Microsoft products (we tried it). Every program has to toe the line.

Simplified networking

Home networking isn't difficult in Windows 95 or 98, but it's not as easy as Windows Me makes it, especially when it comes to getting two or more PCs to share the same internet connection. The clever part of the Windows

Home networking was almost science fiction when Windows 95 was released. Now it's not only possible, it's cheap and easy with Windows Me and a Plug and Play network card.

Me Home Networking Wizard is that it makes you a setup disk you can use on other PCs in a network, even if they're running Windows 95 or 98.

Intelligent help

The Windows help system has been much improved. Windows 98 saw a move towards combining the Windows help system with related system tools and utilities by displaying them side by side. The new Help and Support system in Windows Me goes even further and actually makes some system utilities programs part of Windows Help.

Useful enhancements

System Information – possibly the most useful system tool of all – overlays its menus on the Help and Support screen so that you can use it while still having access to the usual index and search functions of Windows Help. Another innovation is the oddly-named Assisted Support, which logs you onto a website where you can find answers to typical problems. The plan is that PC vendors and third-party manufacturers will be able to add their own system-specific support in the same way.

Digital cameras and scanners

While Windows 98 supports scanners and digital cameras, Windows Me positively welcomes them. You can now preview pictures in a digital camera and selectively download them almost as easily as you'd retrieve pictures from a disk.

There are built-in drivers for many popular cameras, some of which offer better facilities than the ones supplied with the cameras, but the selection of drivers for scanners is limited at present and you may well have to install the one supplied by the

manufacturer, in which case the scanner will work exactly as it always has done with previous versions of Windows.

Interface improvements

Me is the first version of Windows to acknowledge the existence of Zip files as a useful way of compressing and transmitting data. It display Zip files as compressed folders that you can open like ordinary folders. It's even possible to run a program inside a Zip folder without having to decompress it first. The facilities for creating and manipulating Zip folders are not as comprehensive as those in commercial products but it's nice to have them bound into the operating system.

Another cool trick is being able to view many types of graphics files as thumbnails within Windows Explorer. Thumbnails are turned on automatically for My Pictures and you can choose to enable the facility for other folders too. It would have been nice to see this feature extended to other types of file, such as word processed documents and spreadsheets. The Quick View file viewers included with Windows 95 and Windows 98 have been dropped from Windows Me.

The Scanner and Camera Wizard installs itself on a menu only when you add a digital camera or scanner through Control Panel. The Wizard can preview pictures in a camera and save them all in an automatically dated folder with sequential file names.

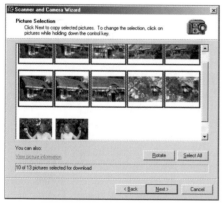

The thumbnail view of files in a folder is a welcome addition to the icon and list views of Windows 95 and Windows 98. The previews are generated surprisingly quickly, even on older PCs.

Games

Games enthusiasts are well catered for by DirectX 7.0, which is the core multimedia component that Microsoft builds into Windows for high-quality sound, music and graphics (although it's already superseded by DirectX 8.0 which you can download from the web). With DirectX 7.0 and a good 3D graphics card Windows Me is a superb environment for exciting games, but you wouldn't think so by looking at what Microsoft provides – 3D Pinball, first seen in the Windows 95 Plus! Pack but now included with the standard Windows Me. Other old friends, including Solitaire and Hearts, are also in attendance. The only new gaming features are internet versions of five board and card games. These are not played against the computer but against a human opponent whom you confront by connecting to the Microsoft Network Game Zone.

We have to admit to a fondness for Space Cadet 3D Pinball but it's hardly state-of-the-art gaming.

Accessibility

Windows Me has a number of features to make it more accessible to people with sight, hearing or co-ordination problems. Many of

The accessibility features of Windows Me are no substitute for the specially-designed accessories available for disabled users, but for silver surfers and anybody with minor physical impairments they're a boon.

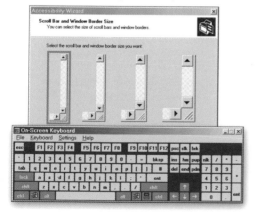

these, such as the screen magnifier, audible warnings and a Wizard to help you design a high-visibility screen layout have been carried over from Windows 98. In addition, there's now an excellent on-screen keyboard suitable for users who have no other way of controlling a PC than with a mouse. Not only does it offer a point and click emulation of a real keyboard, it can also be used by people who are unable to click mouse buttons thanks to a 'hover' mode, in which holding the cursor over a screen key for long enough (one second by default) is deemed to be a click.

Hardware Requirements

The hardware requirements of Windows Me (below) are not particularly onerous. Many older PCs can meet them, and it's impossible to find a new PC that can't. Strictly speaking you don't need a modem but you'll miss a lot without one, and we'd recommend a minimum of 64Mb of RAM.

VGA or higher resolution monitor
150MHz Pentium processor; 32Mb of RAM
480Mb–645Mb free hard disk space
CD-ROM drive
28.8K modem with internet connection
Sound card with speakers or headphones
Mouse or pointing device

Should you upgrade to Windows Me?

On the Microsoft website are ten reasons for upgrading to Me. It would have been nice if the first three had been that it's fast, bug-free and totally reliable, but top of the list is that you can import and edit your own movies; second is that you can move your family pictures from a shoebox to the web; third is that you can archive and index your favourite music.

Perhaps these are Microsoft's idea of a joke because if you want to edit home movies you don't buy a new operating system, you buy a movie editing program – and Windows Movie Maker is in any case more of a novelty than a serious application.

When it comes to family pictures, there's nothing wrong with storing them in a shoebox or the hard disk of a PC where they'll be much more accessible than on the web, and music collections are best archived on media designed for the purpose: tapes, minidiscs and recordable CDs. Admittedly you can use the web to acquire MP3 music files and download them to a portable player, but you can do the same with other versions of Windows too.

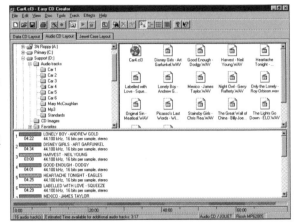

Microsoft's claim that you can store CD-quality audio files on your PC is true, but to transfer them to disc so you can listen to them in the car or on an ordinary CD player requires software that is not included with Me.

Driver support

The lack of drivers in Windows Me has led to complaints from buyers hoping to do a clean install. In the past, a good reason for upgrading to a new version of Windows was better support for existing hardware. Many users upgraded from Windows 95 to Windows 98, and even from the first edition of Windows 98 to the second, solely to get a full set of up-to-date and efficient drivers for their hardware. In Windows Me all this has changed. The best way to install it is as an upgrade to Windows 95 or Windows 98. During a clean install Windows Me will fail to detect even the most ordinary components. If you must do a clean install – this is the only way of switching from Windows 3.1, NT or 2000 – you'll need a full set of up-to-date drivers for every item of hardware in your PC.

There's a fund of informative material relating to Windows Me on Microsoft's website but the rest of the internet community seems to be adopting a wait-and-see attitude.

Should you upgrade to Windows Me?

Missing features

Given how long Windows has been around, and recalling several well-publicised scares that have brought the problems of computer viruses to everyone's attention, it's perhaps surprising that Microsoft does not provide embedded virus protection. This would be far better implemented at operating system level than added on later by third parties.

Also there's no support for recordable (CD-R) or rewritable (CD-RW) drives. They're currently in the list of hot add-ons for PCs, yet users have to rely on third-party software to make them work. Support for them would surely have been in line with the Windows Me emphasis on digital media and entertainment.

Pros and cons

Just after its launch Windows Me is being offered by mail order and online vendors at less than £33 (plus VAT), but only as an upgrade to Windows 98. Windows 95 upgrades are around £59 (plus VAT) and the full retail package is £115 (plus VAT).

There are some good features in Windows Me but nothing you can't emulate in Windows 98 with free downloads from Microsoft and a few well-chosen utilities such as a Zip manager and a roll-back tool. What's more, if you've got a stable, reliable version of Windows 98 running on your PC you'd be brave to swap it for one that's as yet unproven. Even with its new system protection facilities we managed to crash Windows Me several times during the preparation of this book. If you're running Windows 95 on a modern PC with USB ports and a big hard disk you're missing out on 32-bit file access and many Plug and Play features. It's probably worth the upgrade to Windows Me, though you'll have to grit your teeth as you hand over the £59 (plus VAT) and an

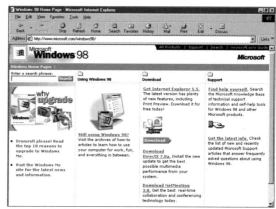

Many of the features of Windows Me, including version 7.0 of Windows Media Player and the latest incarnation of DirectX (for games and multimedia) can be downloaded free from the web, but it's a lot more convenient to fold your arms and let Windows Me install itself from CD.

upgrade to Windows 98 would be just as worthwhile.

Anybody serious about upgrading should bear in mind that Windows 95 and Windows 98 both had to be revamped a year after release, and that a completely new Windows (codenamed Whistler) is promised for late 2001. It promises to cast off the shackles of DOS and provide unprecedented reliability, but Whistler only exists on paper and Windows Me is here now.

Windows Me contains a new version (5.5) of Internet Explorer, but little is new apart from a revised tutorial.

Installing Windows Me - step by step

If you decide to make the switch to Windows Me, take our advice and install it over the top of your existing version of Windows 95 or 98. Provided all the hardware inside your PC is working properly and being correctly identified by your current version of Windows, installing Windows Me is almost a hands-off activity.

So well behaved is the installer that we were able to grab the screens for these steps, paste them into Paint Shop Pro and save them during the upgrade from Windows 98 to Windows Me. We don't recommend that you try the same thing, but it's a testament to the stability of the entire process.

1 Most of the hard work is preparation. Obviously you'll check that your hardware is capable of running Windows Me (see requirements printed on page 85). You should also visit the Microsoft web site at www.microsoft.com/windowsME/upgrade/compat/ to see if your hardware has been tested and approved. Just because your equipment isn't listed doesn't mean it won't work with Windows Me. You'll just have to try it and see.

2 Check that every component in your PC is working properly by opening the System Properties box and clicking the Device Manager tab (see page 38). There should be no exclamation marks or crossed out items. Visit the websites of your graphics card,

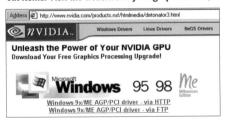

sound card and modem manufacturers to see if there are any driver updates or messages about Windows Me compatibility.

3 Run a full virus check of all the files on your PC, then completely disable the virus checker. If you have a second hard disk or a removable drive, make a full backup of your Windows drive before installing Me. If you haven't got the equipment for this, at least copy any important documents onto floppy disks.

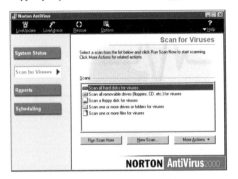

4 Disable any utilities or programs that load as Windows starts, then close down and reboot your PC to make sure they don't reload themselves. If you can't work out how to stop them doing this, uninstall them. If you've bought an upgrade version of Windows Me you may be asked to insert your old Windows CD-ROM to prove your upgrade entitlement. So, keep it handy. Put the Windows Me CD-ROM in the drive and it quickly detects the presence of an older version of Windows and offers to install itself. Click Yes.

5 You'll have to wait a short time until the Windows Me Setup Wizard is ready for action. You will then be prompted to quit all other programs,

which you should already have done, and you can't proceed until you have provided the Windows Me product key, which you'll find on the back of the plastic CD case.

6 The Setup Wizard spends a few minutes checking your PC and preparing some temporary folders for its own use. You're then asked to whether you'd like the Wizard to save your existing system files. It would be foolish not to accept this offer, unless

you've made a full system backup and you know how to use it. If you accept it adds only a few minutes to the installation time but you'll have the security that if Windows Me doesn't like your PC, you can turn back the clock to your old version of Windows.

7 Your next task is to let Windows Me make you a Startup disk. You should already have one of these for your existing version of Windows but the Windows Me one is more important. There's no Exit

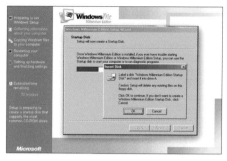

to DOS option in Windows Me so this disk is the only way to start your PC if Windows Me won't work properly. You'll need a new or used disk. Everything already on it will be erased.

8 That's it as far as you're concerned. Once the Setup Wizard starts copying files you might as well take a break. The 'What's new in Me' slide show is unlikely to hold

your attention for long. Installation takes around an hour and involves several reboots. When it's over you'll have to sit through the Welcome to Windows video, which can't be skipped. It's actually not bad but, of course, you're aching to try things out by now.

9 This is the last obstacle before you're let loose on the Windows Me Desktop. If you don't want to watch any of the four self-promoting presentations hit the Exit button in the top right corner to start work (or play). You can come back to this screen at any time.

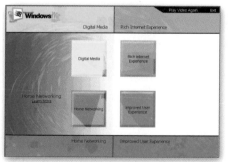

Jargon buster

B Boot To boot (or boot up) a PC is to switch it on and wait for it to start. To reboot is to close it down and then boot it again.

Browser Software program for using the internet.

C Cache An area of memory set aside for storing information so it can be quickly retrieved.

CD-R Compact disc recordable. Blank CDs onto which information can be recorded once. A special CD-R drive is required to make them but a CD drive can play them.

CD-ROM A version of the CD which can store any kind of data, not just music. It stores up to 650Mb of data.

CD-RW Compact disc rewritable. Like CD-R but the information on a CD-RW disc can be erased or changed.

Celeron A budget processor made by Intel. Based on the Pentium III but not as fast.

Clip art Ready made pictures to insert into your own documents.

Context menu The menu that appears when you hold down the right mouse button over a selection, option or file. The menu is context-sensitive because it changes according to the task in hand.

Crash Any situation that causes your PC to stop working properly and forces you to restart it.

D Dialog box A small window which contains a message and/or options for you to make changes to a program or give instructions to Windows.

DMA Dynamic Memory Access.

Document A broad term covering every type of work you can produce with a soft ware program, including spreadsheets, letters, data files, pictures etc.

Download To obtain a file from a website and transfer it to your PC, usually by clicking a word or icon on the web page.

Driver A program (usually small) that acts as an intermediary between Windows and a piece of hardware, passing information between them.

DVD-ROM DVD stands for Digital Versatile Disc. It stores massive amounts of data on a disk that looks like an ordinary CD-ROM. Used mainly for distributing movies with high quality video and audio.

E E-commerce Selling goods and services on the internet.

Email Electronic mail is a way of sending and receiving messages using the internet or a closed network (intranet).

F FAQ Frequently Asked Questions. A file containing the answers to the questions everybody asks at least once.

Favorites/Bookmarks Your address book of links to favourite websites (or documents on your hard disk). Bookmark a site and you can jump straight to it later.

File extension The second part of a file's name, separated from the first part by a dot. It tells Windows what the file is for.

Folder A section of a hard disk where you can store related items. Folders can be created and erased as the need arises.

Freeware Software, often downloadable from the internet, which is then free for you to keep and use.

G Gb (see gigabyte).

Gigabyte A measurement of memory, so big that it's only used to describe the size of hard disks. 1Gb is a thousand megabytes – enough to store a bookcase full of information.

Graphics card A card that fits into an expansion slot inside a PC (and can thus be changed). It generates the screen image.

H Hard disk The main storage in a PC for programs and data.

Home page The first page you see when visiting a website.

I ISP Internet Service Provider. A company that provides you with access to the internet.

K Kilobyte (Kb) A measurement of memory capacity but more often used to describe the size of a file or document. One kilobyte is just over a thousand characters/digits.

M Mailbox The folder in your email application that receives your incoming messages.

Megabyte (Mb) A measurement of memory capacity. 1Mb can store roughly a million alphabetic characters.

Memory Something of an over-used word in computing, it's any form of storage – including hard drives, disks, CD-ROMs and storage chips. The headline memory figure that you see in PC adverts (usually 32Mb–128Mb) is the capacity of its main memory chips.

Modem A device that converts electronic signals from your PC into sounds that can be sent down a phone line.

MP3 A standard means of compressing music so that it requires less storage space but loses hardly any quality.

MS-DOS (DOS) The textbased operating system that everybody used before Windows.

N Newsgroups Discussion groups on the net where you can leave public messages on set topics.

O Online If you're online, you're connected to the internet.

Operating system The operating system software (e.g. Windows) is what controls the actions of the different parts of your PC.

P Partition Result of formatting a hard disk in a special way so it looks like more than one disk.

Pentium A top-range processor made by Intel. The current version is Pentium III.

Peripheral An accessory or add-on, such as a printer or scanner, that plugs into a PC.

Plug and Play Standard devised by Intel to automate the installation and configuration of new computer hardware.

Jargon buster

POP3 An email account that can be accessed remotely from any where over the internet.

Port A socket or connector on the back of a PC into which accessories can be plugged.

Processor Usually called the 'brain' of a PC, although actually it's just the part that does the computing.

R Reboot (See boot).

Refresh rate The image on a computer's screen is constantly redrawn. Refresh rate, expressed in Hertz (Hz) tells you how many times per second.

Registry A central record, kept by Windows, of the way that a PC is configured.

Resolution A measure of the number of dots that make up the picture on a computer screen. The more dots, the sharper the picture.

S Search engine A special type of internet web page where you can type words or phrases and be told on which other internet

pages they can be found.

Serial port An interface to plug in devices such as a modem or mouse to your PC.

Shareware Software that's free to download for an evaluation – if you continue to use it, though, you must pay for it.

Shortcut An icon providing an easier way of starting a program than finding it on a hard disk. It's a sort of pointer to where a file is stored. Find them on the Windows Desktop and in Windows Explorer.

Sound card An add-on device that plugs into a socket inside a PC to provide audio output.

T Taskbar The bar running along the bottom of the Windows Desktop, which displays any active programs. It also holds the Start button.

U URL Uniform Resource Locator, this is the (unique) address of a web page on the internet.

USB Universal Serial Bus connectors are a new standard means of connecting accessories such as scanners and printers to a PC.

W Web-cam Camera that links to a website and displays frequently updated images.

Windows desktop The 'home screen' of Windows. It's what you see when Window starts.

Wizard An automated feature in Windows that guides you through a task or activity.

Z Zip drive A high-capacity disk drive. Available in two versions using pocket-sized removable disks (can store 100Mb or 250Mb).

Zip file Nothing to do with Zip drives. A Zip file is one that has been compressed to save space, and before being used it would have to be expanded. Because Zip files are smaller than the originals they cost less to send over the internet.

Index

Index